Dear Vicki,

May your days be filled with happiness and peace!

Fr Jesse Vog

A Cure For Heartburn:

Discovering and Fulfilling Your Deepest Desire

By Fr. Joshua John Wagner S.T.B., M.A.

Dedication:

This book is dedicated to all those who have aided me in my personal and spiritual formation.

My Parents and Family
My Friends

My Teachers

My Spiritual Directors
Especially Fr. Thomas Radloff S.J.

A Cure For Heartburn: Discovering and Fulfilling Your Deepest Desire

Table of Contents

My Favorite Quote, Ever.

"There is no safe investment. To love at all is to be vulnerable. Love anything and your heart will be wrung, and possibly broken. If you want to make sure of keeping it intact, you must give your heart to no one, even an animal. Wrap it up carefully with hobbies and little luxuries; avoid all entanglements; lock it up safe in the casket or coffin of your own selfishness. But in that casket- safe, dark, motionless, airless- it will change. It will not be broken; it will become unbreakable, impenetrable, irredeemable. The alternative to tragedy, or at least to the risk of tragedy, is damnation. The only place outside of Heaven where you can be perfectly safe from all the dangers and perturbations of love, is Hell."

C.S. Lewis, "The Four Loves."

A Cure For Heartburn
www.FatherWagner.com

A Cure for Heartburn

As a young lad growing up in the United States in the 20th centuries I was given privileges that no other youth in the world are afforded. Certainly, I can say that I got a great education, or lived in a great house, or had the ability and freedom to worship as my family and I had desired. Clearly, the amenities of growing up in America are clear, especially when you go to a country where those things are absent.

Keeping all that in mind, possibly one of the greatest privileges of growing up in the United States- one that still brings me happy memories to this day, was the fact that we had the greatest Taco restaurant the world has ever seen. Taco Bell.

That's right. I said Taco Bell. I have lived in foreign countries- tasted the finest wines, partaken in the most succulent fares- but there is just something about wrapping your hands around a piping hot chilli-cheese burrito, or a double stuffed Taco that just makes you feel all warm and fuzzy inside. Something that comforts you in times of need, and helps you to celebrate the milestones of life, such as getting off work.

Of course, there is a price to pay for all that. Heartburn.

Not only that, but Taco Bell, as good as it is, cannot be the only thing that we eat- it will never TRULY satisfy what our body really needs. Don't get me wrong, it is worth it- but I always have to rely on my old friend Tums, or Pepcid, or good old Pepto Bismol to get me through the rest of the day.

Life though is no different. Certainly there is nothing wrong with partaking in something that brings us pleasure, but it really doesn't cure what makes our hearts burn. Sometimes it makes the "heart burn" worse.

This heart burn I speak of is what is at the deepest desires of every human heart. What makes our hearts burn is the desire to love, and to be loved. To be the best versions of ourselves that we can be. To grow, to learn, and to be better at the end of the day than we were at the beginning of the day. There isn't anything in the world- no pleasure, no amount of success, no amount of "things" -that will cure our heartburn. Only good relationships- being connected spiritually, loving ourselves, and and other human beings can really cure what ails us.

Every relationship can teach us something about love. So can, I hope this book. Using some of my own adventures through life- learning to love myself and others, I hope that my own personal journey learning how to love will help you to establish and maintain those relationships in life that can cure what your

A Cure For Heartburn
www.FatherWagner.com

hearts truly burn for.

A Little Deviation at the Beginning Can Mean Big Trouble at the End: Life Requires Maintenance.

A few years ago, my Boy Scout Troop went on one of our patented camp outs. I used to love camp outs, simply because it always gave us the excuse and the opportunity to eat chilli. Chilli was a staple of our Boy Scout Troop. It was tasty, it was easy to make, and it was always entertaining to feed a bunch of teenage boys chilli. The chilli we made was like chilli salad- we would all bring a can of our favorite chilli, and mix the different cans into one big pot, and create the world's greatest chilli. Add some cheese and Frito's and you had yourself a fine meal my friends.

Oddly, this story is not about Chilli. I just wanted to share my love of chilli with all of my readers. At the particular camp out, we were going to study orienteering. Orienteering is the navigation of terrain using a compass and a map. I am particularly notorious for my bad sense of direction, so giving me a map and compass could only lead to disaster.

The way that the camp out worked was that we were supposed to navigate a series of way points using the map and the compass. We broke into groups, each having its own set of way points and goals- the first to arrive at the final way point, which was the same for all the groups, won the competition. I will just say, as a matter of dramatic irony, that we did not win the competition.

So we started out navigating the course- I was the compass guy in our group, and we were supposed to find a direction and go so many feet or miles or whatever we were supposed to do. From that point, we would find the next set of coordinates and so on. Let's say that the direction was 252 degrees, or west(ish). Being the type of guy that I am, I found 250, told the guys which direction to go and we were off.

Boy, were we off.

We were way off.

We never found the first way point in fact. We spent the next couple of hours trying to figure out where we were and where we were supposed to be. Finally, we realized that we had started off on the wrong foot- the fact that I found 250 and not 252 made all the difference. At first, we were pretty much on course, but as we went further on, that little 2 degree difference made all the difference. After a couple of miles we were almost a mile off course.

We finally had our leader help us out, and we found

A Cure For Heartburn
www.FatherWagner.com

the final way point, simply because he knew where it was. There was still chilli to be eaten there, don't worry!

Boy how we can be like that sometimes. We think we are generally going in the right direction, but a couple of degrees off at the beginning, and we could end up way off course. I had a boss once tell me that God is in the details. Or was it the Devil? Either way... it may seem that we have gone in the right direction at first, but it is horrible to find that we are way off route at the end.

Our problem with the orienteering was that we just set off in a direction and assumed that we were on the right track the whole time. We went in a straight line and assumed that everything would turn out right. Life is never about a straight route though; as often we must zig and zag, and constantly correct the course we are on to make sure that we arrive at our final destination.

A great analogy I once heard is an air plane. Most of us, when we fly, assume that the air plane is travelling in a straight line, from point A to point B. It turns out that an air plane is rarely on course, though. In fact, an air plane is on course less than 10% of the time. A plane's route is more like a zigzag or a wavy type pattern. If the plane didn't constantly make course corrections, the flight from LA to Chicago, it would end up in Tucson!

Our lives have to operate in a similar manner. We simply can't point ourselves in a particular direction and expect that we are going to arrive at our destination. Even a little deviation at the beginning can mean that we will almost always miss the mark at the end.

Our lives require a daily course correction- we have to see where we are coming from, where we are, and if we are still heading in the right direction- in other words our lives are in constant need of course correction, much like the route of an air plane. The quickest way to get between two points is a straight line, but rarely do straight lines exist in real life. It is so much better to make those course corrections early rather than find out just how far off the mark you are at the end!

Much like the pilots of an air plane, or Boy Scouts on the trail, we need to constantly monitor ourselves to make sure we get to whatever destination we desire to arrive at. Certainly it takes a lot of work and focus, but the results are always worth it.

The final piece of the puzzle is that we have to trust the instruments provided to us to navigate our way through life. Just like the pilot has to trust his control panel, and the Boy Scout his compass, so we have to trust the instruments in our lives- people, places, and structures that are external to ourselves to help us make sure that we are on route. Our relationship

A Cure For Heartburn
www.FatherWagner.com

with God, counsellors, pastors, life coaches, mentors, support groups, friends, and family members are all good resources for us to trust in our journey of life to help us be accountable to them and ourselves to maximize the possibility for success.

That means we have to find and establish relationships with people that we trust to point us in the right direction, to put us back on course, and arrive safely at our destination, whatever that might be, and listen to the advice and guidance they give us.

Instant Gratification Doesn't Always Mean Instant Success

When I was a kid I rarely got mail. I am not sure that there are many kids that get a lot of mail, although I am sure that since even 3 year olds have email now, they at least get the same Spam from the widows of African Generals who just need to borrow my bank account for a little while, so that she can get her money out of Zimbabwe. (By the way, I am still waiting on my 10% cut of that 28 million dollars.) (I am sure it won't be long before it comes. In the meantime, I guess they needed to max out my checking account to help with the transfer.)

When I was a kid, I received one of the greatest letters in the mail that I possibly could: It was from my good friend, Ed. McMahon. That's right, even though I had only vaguely heard of him and never met him, he sent me... ME... a letter with the greatest message a kid could read: I had won a million dollars!

I was already driving a monster truck in my mind's eye. It had flames on the side.

All I had to do was to submit the entry form to claim my prize of one million dollars (as I type this, I am putting my pinkie up to my mouth, a-la Dr. Evil). I knew that all my problems were over... no more need for an allowance, and I could probably buy off my parents and brothers... probably.

I sent in the envelope and waited for Ed to show up with my check. I waited a long time. Almost as long as I am waiting for that General's widow to deposit that money into my account... where the heck is she??!

Finally, the day came... again I got something in the mail. I figured that Ed was busy and couldn't personally deliver my check- probably he was busy delivering other people's checks I was sure... Did he even live in Ohio? What I got in the mail wasn't a check though- it was a subscription to a golfing magazine.

I have never golfed.

I will never golf.

All of my dreams of monster trucks and gold plated toilets slipped through my fingers. Maybe I could golf my way to millions. I was just a regular kid again... I would have to earn it if I wanted a million dollars.

You know, I would love to find some way to get rich quick... who the heck wouldn't? While I am at it, I would love to find some way to lose weight quickly without any personal risk. Oh yea, I would love to be world famous too... by tomorrow.

I have a sneaking suspicion that I am not alone in

these and similar sentiments. I love instant gratification- I love getting something for nothing- no work, no investment, no pain or commitment.

Why do you think guys keep selling schemes to make money (why would they be selling it if it worked so well? Seems you would want to keep it a secret.) How about all the fad diets and pills and procedures that help us to lose weight quickly? Not that I am against them, or think they are bad or immoral, but I doubt that it gets to the root of why most people eat.

If we want something worthwhile- a true balance in our lives, it is not something that happens in an instant, but something we grow into. It requires work to do- sometimes it is easy and other times it isn't. I wish I could find that equilibrium instantly, but I doubt it would be equilibrium at all. Usually, instant gratification comes with consequences- I know that all the fad diets I have ever tried, I end up gaining more weight than I ever lost. I am sure that most of those people that take part in investment schemes end up losing their money, simply because for those schemes to work requires a full time job, and that is contrary to the message that sold them the product in the first place.

I guess there are two ways to look at this analogously. It is sort of like robbing a bank- yea you get money instantly, but the consequences are dire- jail, death, or the endangering of other people. No bank robber robs banks just because it is evil by the way, but there is something good they get out of it instantly- the thrill, quick money etc. In the same way, no one who takes drugs takes them because it will destroy their bodies, but for the instant feeling it gets them.

The better way to do it is to get a job and work for it- to struggle and to save little by little. Certainly the money won't come as quickly, but neither will the consequences. I have a feeling that a person who understands this appreciates every hard earned pay check that they make.

When it comes to anything else, the same thing works- if you lose weight one pound a week, you have a tendency to keep it off, because you give yourself time to change your habits. Money, or houses, or whatever rightly earned is always more fulfilling than getting it quickly through schemes or robbery. Dealing with how we feel is much better than suppressing it with drugs or alcohol or shopping or whatever addiction makes us feel temporarily better. You still need to deal with the consequences of those feelings, as well as others associated with the addiction, once the drug wears off.

I still fight this need for instant gratification- it is part of our culture- instant cameras, cell phone that contact other people instantly- air planes that can fly around the world in a matter of hours. I can tell you from my own experience, that when we do the work and take the time, the outcome is always more fulfilling.

The Myth of Perfection: If You Want to Live, You Have to Grow

Before last January, I haven't run more than about 12 feet since I was about 12 years old. Running is a hard thing to do for me- you have to sweat for one. Of course, I don't sweat, rather I glow. My glowing is really wet and stinky though.

I have always been a big fan of walking though, and one day after Thanksgiving I ended up walking about 12 miles, for no other reason than I had enough time off to walk 12 miles. Having done that, a friend of mine told me that I should learn how to run, and train for the Columbus half marathon in April of last year.

PREPOSTEROUS I thought. Me? A Runner? I have a hard enough time walking without falling off of the side walk, let alone trying to do that quickly, in a city, surrounded by 10,000 strangers. I scoffed at the idea, but eventually acquiesced, and began to train for the marathon.

I started by walking fast, then faster, and even ran about 13 feet, a personal record set for me in Mrs. Thomas' 5th grade gym class, not to be broken until I was nearly 30 years old. Eventually, that 13 feet

A Cure For Heartburn
www.FatherWagner.com

turned into a mile, which turned into 2,3,4, and toward the end of my training 12 miles! I couldn't believe it! Every week I would just add a mile to what I had done the week before, so it wasn't as tedious and mentally challenging which is really what turned me off of running in the first place.

The day of the big race came, and I was psyched! It was cold and rainy that day, but I was determined to combat the elements and run a good race. As we began, I ran at an even pace, because I knew that the race was long. One foot in front of the other. Sure there was a little tightness in my hamstrings, but I was able to persevere!

I ran the 10k portion of the 13.2 mile race, which works out to roughly half of a half marathon, in about an hour and six minutes- not too shabby for a guy running his first marathon. Then it happened.

My hamstrings locked up in the 7th mile... and I had to walk. I was so disappointed in myself! I had done all this training for months and months, and I had to walk!!!! So I walked the 7th mile, waiting for my hamstrings to loosen up.

After a little while, I began to jog again, and even pick up a little speed, so that I finished in just under 2 and a half hours. I was so upset at myself. I was so upset that I didn't run the perfect race. I couldn't see the fact that I had just travelled, by foot, 13 miles. I don't

A Cure For Heartburn
www.FatherWagner.com

even like to drive 13 miles! I couldn't see that I had gone from walking to running in a matter of months. I couldn't see the other 12 miles that I had run- just that one stinkin' mile that I had to walk. 3 months of training destroyed by one mile.

We can all be like that I think. A lot of us anyway. American culture both chases and loathes perfection. For some reason the culture has come to expect perfection in its people- if you aren't perfect, then you aren't wanted. So we are told that we need to be perfect. On the other hand, we love it when so- called "perfect" celebrities, or politicians fall flat on their face and fail- maybe because it makes us feel a little better about our own imperfections. I dunno, maybe it is just me who is a perfectionist.

Perfection in this life is simply impossible! At least with a definition of perfection that is common and popular- that is a person with no physical or emotional flaws- a person without any character defects. No one like that exists- not even Oprah or Dr. Phil!

But "perfection" in another sense is possible. Trees are perfect in a sense- trees are perfect insofar as they are constantly growing. If a tree stops growing, it is one step away from dying, or it is already dead. Trees are perfect as long as they are doing what they are supposed to do, and that is to grow. It they aren't growing they are dying.

A Cure For Heartburn
www.FatherWagner.com

Trees go through a lot of changes while they grow. They have to endure the wind and the rain, they need sunlight, they have to lose their leaves, and put down their roots despite the hardness of the soil. They have to lose bark, and grow new layers. Growth for a tree can be serious work!

We aren't really any different. We have been designed to grow in whatever environment we have been placed in. If we stop growing, and learning, that means that we are one step away from dying, perhaps spiritually and emotionally, if not physically. Growing is what we have been made to do.

Growth for us human beings can be tough though, just like it is for the tree. It requires us to leave behind places, habits, and even people who may have been important to us at one time. It means that sometimes there will be growing pains. It means not being so hard on ourselves for our perceived "imperfections," and seeing them as opportunities for growth.

Sometimes when you look at the rings on the tree you can see that some years had better and faster growth than others- we aren't different. There are times in which we will grow quickly, and other times when it doesn't seem like we are growing at all.

It can hurt to grow, but if a tree doesn't grow it can't produce fruit because it is dead. So our growth lets us be something greater than we are now, potentially.

A Cure For Heartburn
www.FatherWagner.com

I know that I can look back on life and see events that weren't pleasant, but helped to make me grow into the person I currently am.

So I guess that the word perfection is something of a misunderstood term- it is misunderstood what it means. The word that we really should be talking about is progress.

In this life, I like to say, perfection equals progress.

Like the tree that is perfect when it does what it is supposed to, namely grow, so we are perfect only when we are growing.

When I think of that marathon last year, and the accomplishments I made in going from not running, to running most of a half marathon I am astounded. If all I focus on is that 7th mile that I had to walk, I am depressed. Rather, I should look at that 7th mile as an opportunity to grow and become even better and faster- as something to reach for, just like a tree reaches for the sun!

A Cure For Heartburn
www.FatherWagner.com

Love and Fear

A few years ago, I was able to help a local high school participate in a "ropes course." A ropes course is something lets lets us all bring out the "Inner Tarzan." I guess some people can have an "Inner Jane" as well, or some mixture of both Tarzan and Jane. I am sure if that happens, there is a lot of internal conflict and strife, and in any case, a whole lot of swinging going on. I myself have an inner "Cheeta." (Cheeta is the name of the monkey that the movie Tarzan had with him.) (I do love monkeys.)

I have digressed so much from my first sentence, I think I may have forgotten what I was talking about... oh yea, the ropes course. Anyway, the ropes course is a set of, well, ropes set way up high in the sky, about 40-75 feet up. It is a set of cables and nets and obstacles ranging from trapeze, to tight ropes, and zip cords. As I mentioned, the catch is that this is all suspended anywhere from 40 to 75 feet in the sky.

While I was there with the high school group, I watched as these kids attempted to fly through the sky on the various obstacles. The point of this exercise, apart from being a good way to get out of biology class, is meant to teach teamwork, and, I guess, how to be really afraid of heights. I never ventured on to the ropes course, as truly I do not have an inner monkey, rather I have an inner chicken. (OK, I admit, it is more of an inner turkey... gobble gobble.) (Hamburgler: Rubble, Rubble)

Of course, this completely sounds insane. Teenagers should probably not even be allowed to drive, let alone frolic tens of feet above the harsh, unforgiving ground. There is a catch though- while there is no net to catch them if they miss the trapeze bar, or fall off of the zip cord, every person who is doing the ropes course has a safety harness on, with two safety wires attached to strong steel cables which run over the top of every one of the obstacles.

So the fear is really just perceived fear, as if you fail an obstacle, you won't really fall to a gruesome death and ruin the prom, but you will be safely tethered, twice, to cables strong enough to hold a bridge together.

It was interesting to watch which kids trusted the safety cables and which ones didn't. For the most part, nobody could really fall- the ones that realized that had fun on the course, going from obstacle to obstacle, while the other kids who didn't trust in the cables would perch on the side of the upright poles which held the course, and never venture out into the high wire, the zip cord, or anything else. The kids that trusted in their safety harness could certainly do just about anything they wanted on the ropes course.

A Cure For Heartburn

It was interesting how there was very little middle ground for those kids; they either you loved it, or were terrified by it. There were some (like me) who wouldn't even climb the poles in the first place.

Our lives work like that. Fear. Fear is a great motivating factor- but it is irrational, telling us that there is danger when there really isn't any to be found. Fear shouldn't be confused with prudence.

Prudence is a total rational thing, which tells us when something is good to do, or when to avoid a potentially dangerous situation.

Fear is always irrational. Certainly, sometimes it can serve a good purpose, such as avoiding those afore mentioned dangerous situations, but a lot of the time is makes us do really, really silly things to ourselves.

There are a lot of things to fear- fear of death, fear of economic insecurity, fear of rejection. There are even times when we might be afraid of how we feel, or even of memories. We can be afraid to acknowledge the past, or fear looking at the future. Fear comes in a lot of shapes and sizes. Fear can prevent us from taking risks that we should be taking, and can even move us away from success- I know people that are afraid to succeed!

Fear is an emotion that is hard to battle- I think a lot of people struggle with it- everyone struggles with it

A Cure For Heartburn
www.FatherWagner.com

in one way or another, and we have all tried to run from it from time to time, one way or another.

I have heard FEAR spells out two acronyms: "Forget Everything And Run," and "Future Events Appearing Real." Both are good acronyms for fear, as fear is always ALWAYS irrational. Like those kids on the ropes course who didn't believe in the safety wires, it can paralyse us, even when the fear isn't really justified.

The opposite of fear is love- love is always rational. Love is always choosing and willing the good of ourselves and another, despite how we might feel at a particular moment. Fear and love are exclusive terms, where there is love, fear cannot exist, simply because good rational love- doing what is good and right- is always more powerful than fear. Love is not simply the desire to do something good, it is actually doing it, and knowing it is the right thing to do, despite "feeling" fear or anxiety. Fear is an emotion- love is an action.

If we go back to that ropes course analogy, love would be the two safety wires attached to the cables above every obstacle. See, the difference here between love and fear become apparent- fear is the intangible feeling felt when we are way up in the ropes course- love is the real and tangible wires that will never let us fall, as long as we stay attached.

If the person doing the ropes course removed their safety harness or wires, and then attempted to do the course, that would be reckless imprudence- but as long as they are tethered, they can do just about anything they want- the same is true with love. Since love is an action, it can also be a habit- something that we continually do over and over again becomes easier and more natural over time, enabling us to trust more deeply, and love more thoroughly.

Why two wires? The two wires in our analogy represent the two types of relationships that we need to ensure that we are happy and healthy people. One of the wires is our relationship with a higher power, namely God, and the other represents good and right ordered relationships with other people.

It is interesting when two people are on the same obstacle in the ropes course, they are tethered to the same safety cable- so they are really tethered together in a sense- what protects one, protects the other. They are both also able to encourage each other to step out into the particular obstacle, and to trust the safety that has been put into place.

In our lives, as long as we stay tethered in love- real acts of willing the good of another despite our irrational emotions, there is almost nothing that we cannot accomplish. That is why a good spiritual life, and a good social life (both with friends and family) are essential for a happy healthy person. Love allows us to eradicate fear, and do what is best to overcome any obstacle that we might face in the future.

To try and do things by ourselves- even if we are capable- is as insane as doing the ropes course without the safety wires protecting us. Certainly, we might get through one or two obstacles, but eventually if we are by ourselves we will slip and fall to our deaths.

If we wish to overcome fear in our own lives, we have to love, and trust in love- trust that doing the right thing, even if it is difficult, will always bear a lot of fruit, and will always be better than never taking the risk, and staying on the ground with the rest of the turkeys who will never fly.

We should take a moment every day to do maintenance on our relationships, both spiritual and social, because these relationships help to give us not only a context and identity, but the ability to love and overcome fear that might otherwise be holding us back.

Self-Love Vs. Selfishness

When I was in High School and still living at home, we had a Sunday tradition that we engaged in religiously. We would all get up in the morning, go to Mass at St. Paul's church in Westerville, Ohio (know in those days simply as the 'Ville) (OK, I was the only one who called it that) (Thought it made me look more Urban) (Pope Urban that is), and after Mass we would truck over to Ryan's Steak house.

For those of you around the world, or the US, who doesn't know who Ryan's Steak house is, it is one of the reasons that people around the world might not like the United States of America. It is one of those places with a buffet a mile long, filled with all sorts of food, from salad to fried chicken, ribs, or whatever you can imagine. And the best part is that they keep bringing out all sorts of new hot items. (As a side note, you are apparently NOT supposed to just go up to the buffet line and stick your face in the mashed potato bin. Not only do they get upset, but the butter also tends to scald your face. Just thought I would warn you)

Now I have a philosophy about food: I like it. A lot. I have, to quote Chris Farley, what "Doctors call a bit of weight problem." It is certainly something I struggle with from time to time. So those kind of places are just nightmares for me- any kind of all you can eat place- I feel like I have to get my money's worth when I go in there, and I usually end up feeling bloated and sleepy toward the end of the meal.

There is nothing wrong with eating- nothing wrong with enjoying a meal with some friends, or family- nothing wrong with having a good meal, but there is something wrong with engorging yourself on the buffet line, to the point where an ambulance has to come get you to take you home. I guess this would be a good analogy for the difference between selfishness and self-love.

I think that sometimes these two things get confused. For instance, some people think that doing something nice for themselves is selfishness. Others may think that they are simply taking care of themselves, and it is self-love. I guess it really is a matter of perspective, and relies mostly on your intentions.

The way that we must distinguish self-love from selfishness is not in the act itself, but in the outcome of the act. For instance, if a person takes time off to recharge, regenerate, and spend time with friends and family that is alright. If the effect is that it begins to make their work life deteriorate, or they spend all their time in recreation, then it becomes selfishness.

Drinking isn't bad, but for some people it is a totally

selfish act- the purpose of the drink becomes escaping instead of relaxation. Some people don't have a choice in this, by the way- but the same can happen in terms of anything that we use to relax. Once it crosses the lone and becomes the primary thing we seek after to the neglect of other things, rather than being a support for our relationships and our work life, we have crossed the line over into selfishness.

So what is self-love? It is simply taking care of yourself- doing what is in the highest good for yourself, and something that augments, and does not detract from daily responsibilities and relationships.

I know someone once who had to deal with a particular issue in their lives, to the point where they had to seek out a support group. That person felt incredibly guilty that they had to spend time in the group, and felt that they should be spending time with their family instead. I had to explain to them that by spending time getting help with a particular issue; they would be a better friend, spouse, parent, and member of their community. It wasn't selfish, but self-loving.

The real difference again lies in the intention- self-love always takes into account everyone around us- we do loving things for ourselves IN ORDER THAT we might love those people around us, and fulfil our duties. A nice relaxing day at the beach, watching a ball game or even taking a walk in the park can mean the difference between a person who is a big ball of stress, and the person who is effective and efficient in their lives.

In grad school, we had a professor who reminded us that you can't give what you don't have. That completely applies to every aspect of our lives- For instance, I would love to give you a million dollars, but I just don't have it (yet). The same is true about love- if you don't love yourself how is it possible to love other people? Again, true self-love is really directed away from ourselves- we love ourselves in order that we might love others. Selfishness is simply about pleasing our appetites, and ourselves, running away from personal thoughts and feelings, or even responsibilities and relationships that frighten us, and usually ends up hurting not only us, but also the people around us.

One last note on self-love. It is really hard to do. We are probably the hardest person to love simply because me might not think we are worth loving ourselves, or know how to truly love ourselves. We have to live with our faults, and it is sometimes easier to see those than all the good things we have and are. No matter how "good" or "bad" we might be, we are loveable, we deserve and need to be loved, both from outside and within ourselves.

A Cure For Heartburn
www.FatherWagner.com

The Crisis of Identity- Man's Search for Meaning- Some Reflections on Death

Recently, I had the opportunity to take some time out for a spiritual retreat. I was able to go with one of my dearest and closest friends to a retreat house in Fremont, Ohio, Our Lady of the Pines, run by the Sisters of Mercy. It was a fantastic experience- there is nothing like a place that has been prayed in, and that is one of those places. It reminded me a lot of the place in Morristown New Jersey where I spent thirty days in silence last summer.

Places that have been "prayed in," are obvious. It is sort of like a hotel room that has been smoked in- it is in the walls and in the sheets and the bedding. It is obvious when you first walk into the room that someone has been there who was smoking- in an analogous manner, the feeling that a place has been prayed in is just as obvious- it is in the walls and in the bedding. It soaks into the carpet, and is reflected in the people who live and work there- it is obvious when you walk in, as you smell not the acrid smell of cigarette smoke, but the fragrance of holiness.

I spent the weekend in silence- except for the part where I visited my spiritual director in Toledo- the sun was out and bright (a nice change from the cloud belt of Columbus, Ohio), but there was also snow on the ground. It made things even brighter! On the last day I decided to go for a walk and to shoot some pictures of the grounds and the surrounding area.

I walked through the cemetery where the sisters were buried from the decades past, and saw an even bigger cemetery just across the street. So I mossier over there- I like cemeteries for some reason- I grew up near a giant one in Lima, so I guess I have never felt creepy there or anything like that. Cemeteries tell a lot about the people who lived near them- whole families buried together- some people lived a long time, while others only a few days. A gravestone is sort of like the tip of the iceberg- there is so much more about a person underneath that their marker just can't tell.

One of the striking things about the grave markers though, was the fact that every single last one tells us about a relationship that the person it commemorates had- large or small they all had names on them. Those names denoted a relationship with people of similar names. As I mentioned above, there were whole families- sons, daughters, mothers and fathers- all buried together. Some of the gravestones told of a married couple- the day they were married, the kids they had, when they were born and when they died. Some were just little kids who only lived for a few days, but were never forgotten- even 50 years after her death at the age of 4 days, one person's gravestone read beloved daughter. There were fresh flowers there.

My favorite gravestone didn't have a picture of a family member, or even a picture of Jesus or Mary (it was a Catholic cemetery), but a tow truck- a tow truck with the name Fischer Towing was carved into the side of a gravestone! Must have been his truck.

Certainly gets one to think doesn't it? I mean, as another friend of mine often says, none of us are getting out of here alive. Where is the meaning in our lives? Where do we go when we die? No matter how strong one's faith is that second question is always unknown. The first though, I think can be answered.

A few months back I read Viktor Frankle's book on man's search for meaning, entitled "Man's Search for Meaning." He talked about how he survived the death camps at Auschwitz because he had a meaning and purpose. Those who didn't survive often died because they lost a reason to live. We all need that or we die- we die in our daily actions, in our relationships, and in ourselves without meaning. We are not meant to drift- even the ancient philosophers knew that we had a "final cause," that is, something we are directed towards.

How do we find meaning then? I suspect that is something that we all struggle with- it is the issue of trying to figure out our identity in this life- to give our lives meaning.

Frankle's solution was an interesting one- he said that we have to imagine ourselves on our deathbed, looking back at our lives. What do we want to see there? What would we see if that day was tomorrow? I do not believe that this exercise is intended to be moribund; rather, it is a means to focus ourselves in the direction we are supposed to in life, and the meaning we attach to our identity.

I have a sneaking suspicion that those gravestones I saw were a key to the answer. With the exception of the tow truck guy, nobody had their occupation on their gravestone. But everybody had some reference, even if just a name, to a relationship. Be it to God, or their spouse, or children or parents invariably what defined people were their relationships. That is what gives us identity and meaning- or that is what should.

Even the nuns who were buried there had an R.S.M. after each of their names, denoting a relationship with their order, and the other sisters in it.

My spiritual director told me the story of his uncle who was very rich. He spent his whole life amassing a great deal of wealth- he never married because he was too busy making money. He was a very successful man- when he was in his 60's he had a stroke and was confined to a wheelchair in a (probably very nice) nursing home. My director told me that until the day he died he only said one phrase over and over- "what a rip-off."

So I guess I would challenge you with the same exercise as Victor Frankle- if you were on your deathbed looking back on life, what would you see? What would you want to see? What are the relationships in our lives that give us meaning, and how are they going? The answer to the second question is also the answer to our search for identity, and the search for meaning in our lives.

Only this way will life never become a rip-off.

"Nothing is more practical than finding God, that is, than falling in a love in a quite absolute, final way. What you are in love with, what seizes your imagination will affect everything. It will decide what will get you out of bed in the mornings, what you will do with your evenings, how you spend your weekends, what you read, who you know, what breaks your heart, and what amazes you with joy and gratitude. Fall in love, stay in love, and it will decide everything."- Pedro Arrupe, S.J.

Kobayashi -Maru

(Living with the No-Win Scenario)

There are in fact great moments in movie history that no one will ever forget. For instance, the moment that Clark Gable uttered those famous words in "Gone with the Wind," - "Frankly my dear, I don't give a damn." Or how about in Braveheart when William Wallace yells out "Freedom!" with his last ounce of strength after having been drawn and quartered? What about Jack Nicholas's performance in A Few Good Men? ("You can't handle the truth!")

Certainly these are memorable movie moments, but one that can't simply be expressed by pickout out one lone or scene- a moment that changed movie history- possibly forever...

Star Trek II the Wrath of Khan.

This movie changed my life as a young boy. How could it not change you? HOW I ASK!!?? Not only did you have the great American hero Captain Kirk and his faithful shadow Mr. Spock, (along with Bones McCoy and the other cast members from Star Trek), but you had the greatest Star Trek villain... possibly ever: Ricardo Montalbon as Khan. Kids all around America- nay, the world- wanted a fake chest of their own to wear like him. Could there be a more perfect villain than the guy from Fantasy Island? If there is one, he hasn't been born yet.

Look at those (fake) pecs... KHAAAANN
While I could wax on about this... well, masterpiece of cinematography, I will spare you and get to the point. There is a great opening scene in ST:II that I have used in my life since I first saw it in 1982.

The opening scene has a young Kirstie Alley playing the part of Saavik, the Vulcan protege of Mr. Spock and the conn of the Enterprise. She is commanding in this performance, and thank goodness, because it took all of her might to replace Diane on Cheers just a few years later.

Just then a distress call comes in from the Kobayashi -Maru, some kind of transport ship filled with innocent people. It seems that it hit a mine and is now drifting in Klingon space. Saavik has two choices- leave the people to die at the hands of Klingons, or risk the crew of the Enterprise and enter the territory, opening them up for attack by the superior Klingons.

They of course go in to save the Kobayashi -Maru, and get blown to smitherines. (Well, OK it was just a simulation, but it really look like Uhura bit it this time.)

This is the classic no win scenario. We all have to face the Kobayashi -Maru from time to time- the situation in which any decision we make is going to result in someone getting hurt, or someone losing out. It is the classic not pleasing everyone scenario.

I hate those kinds of decisions. They really happen all the time- to people- to organizations- to businesses- where the good of the whole family or organization has to outweigh at times the good of the individual. Of course there are times as well in which to save a life, one must make a sacrifice.

I would guess that what we are talking about is really love. I have a few definitions of love that are important- they are really a conglomeration of my own experience as well as things I have learned from other people. The two that I will deal with here:

Love is a choice not a feeling
Love is the choice of doing the greatest good for myself and my neighbor

When it comes to these "no-win" situations- where someone or something is going to have to suffer, we have to ask ourselves what the greatest good is in any particular situation. Sometimes the greatest good stinks- it is often painful to do, but if it is the greatest good, it must be done. I guess another definition of love is the pursuit of the greatest good at all costs.

I guess in personal situations, that could mean ending a relationship to preserve greater hurt down the road. Maybe it is the father of a family taking a job in another city that will help the family survive in rough times- perhaps it is laying off 500 people from a factory so that 2000 might not lose their jobs.

I have discovered, especially in the last couple of years, that life is a very messy affair, and is rarely clean cut or clear If love is the pursuit of the good, then courage is the virtue by which we carry out that good- sometimes we just have to fly the shop into Klingon territory just to try- even if it means that no one is going to make it out.

Pursuing the greatest good on an individual or corporate level is a constant balancing act that requires us to think ahead and do what is best- not only for ourselves- but for everyone involved.

I guess there should be a post on here as to what "good" means. That has been a question that goes back to the beginning of philosophy!

The Best Way to Re-Commit: Don't

A couple of years ago, I began a journey- a journey to make myself look, feel, and act, like Arnold Schwarzenegger. I have thus far failed. It turns out I can't even do an Austrian accent, although I have known several Austrians, and have even worked out once in Vienna, I have failed to reach the epic 1970's proportions of everyone's favorite body builder.

When I embarked on that journey, I embarked with a bunch of zeal, and for three straight months, I lifted three times a week, built up my strength and my muscles, and watched the numbers on the sheet I was writing my stats on rise with every week that I lifted. Certainly, I did not turn out like Arnold, but the lifting and the physical exercise made me feel incredible. It is something I try to maintain in one way or another all the time in my life.

It is funny though, after about three months I hit a plateau. The numbers stopped going up as fast, if at all, and I was starting to lose hope that I someday would be Mr. Universe... or Conan the Barbarian. So I re-committed myself to working out harder, pushing myself more, and re-dedicating myself to the workout routine with the same zeal I had started with three months prior.

A Cure For Heartburn
www.FatherWagner.com

That lasted all of a week. I found that I was dragging myself into the gym that I had previously loved, and that my workouts were not all that effective in getting the numbers to go higher. I knew they could go higher but all the re-commitment in the world wasn't working. I couldn't figure out what was wrong- I was doing all the same stuff I had done for the previous three months- things that had gotten me fired up and gotten me results, but to no avail.

Then I realized, that was the problem. I began reading up on this, and I realized that my muscles had gotten used to the same old routine that I had been doing for the last three months, which limited their ability to grow. Not only that, but mentally, I had gotten bored with the routine- so as much as I wanted to re-commit myself, it was growing more difficult, both physically and mentally. I was no longer challenging myself in either aspect, so my workouts became boring and ineffective, no matter how much I wanted to re-commit. There was no way that I was going to do an encore to that previous three months' of workouts.

So I changed it up. I got some more books and changed up my routine- I picked a different set of exercises, a different order to my workout, and even different music than I was listening to before. (I had been listening to the same CD for three months too!) I changed everything. In a sense, I re-committed to my physical well being by not re-committing at all. In fact it was difficult to re-commit to the same old routine, nearly impossible.

I think that this sort of thinking needs to apply to everything. It is very easy to get comfortable in our relationships, our jobs, our spiritual life, or even our intellectual life. When we get comfortable, even with good habits, we can stagnate the growth that we might be capable of doing, simply because it is easier to do. That can make us lazy, and even prone to losing the good habits we might have formed.

The way to re-commit to anything is to totally re-think how you are doing it. There is nothing more fun than starting a new project, to find a new way to look at and examine anything that is out there- new ways to experience a relationship that refreshes and renews it.

As I have mentioned in a previous chapter, if we are not growing we are dead. Certainly the new workout that I established after the first three months was a hard routine to get into- my muscles weren't use to it, it required more concentration, and it forced me to learn how to do the same old thing in a brand new and exciting way. The result- my numbers started to go up on my stat sheet again.

How does this apply to a job? Maybe you can't seem to find fulfilment in a job because you have gotten

A Cure For Heartburn
www.FatherWagner.com

into a rut and can't get out. The same routine is no longer a mental challenge, and you need to look for a new department and new challenges to make you grow.

How about relationships? Maybe you have been married for a while, and things have gotten stale. Look at your routines- maybe you have been doing the same things together that worked twenty years ago. But, you are different people than you were twenty years ago! Things may have changed, and so should the dynamic of your relationships. Maybe it is as simple as trying a new restaurant!

In your spiritual life, perhaps you have prayed and meditated the same way for years, and it once brought a great amount of fruit to your spiritual well being, but these days your prayer has been stale- try a new tact- there are plenty of spiritual devotions and practices that can refresh your relationship with God.

This existence is constantly one of the tensions between trying to stay the same- what is comfortable for us, and what worked for us in the past, verses dealing with the changing nature of the world we live in, and people we are. Somehow we have to balance consistency with challenging ourselves with new ways of thinking and acting so that we can continue to grow and fulfil our potential at this moment of our lives.

As a friend once told me, she likes to do things every so often that gets her out of her comfort zone- she even tried dancing in an advanced jazz class without ever having one jazz dance lesson ever in her life! Getting out of our comfort zones is the first step in establishing a new comfort zone to grow into- certainly that means leaving the past behind, but taking with us that which will make us grow.

I will leave you with this analogy- a plant needs a new flower pot every-so-often in order to continue to grow, or else it will be smothered and die. That doesn't mean that the flowerpot didn't serve its purpose, just that it outgrew the one it was in. To move a plant from one pot to another, or a pot to the ground is tremendously hard and risky on the plant, but the potential for growth is unimaginable!

So how do you re-commit to anything? Throw out the old play book, and write a new one! Commit by not re-committing to whatever makes us too comfortable.

Keep your Focus

"Lack of Focus is Death"... that is a saying that I heard once at a conference. Lack of focus is dangerous... It got me to thinking about a professor I knew in Rome. I can't remember her name (which is probably a good thing,) but I knew that she taught philosophy in English to a few English-speaking students in town. I never had her myself as a teacher, but met her in a coffee bar in one of the universities I attended in Rome.

I was startled to hear how badly she spoke English- I knew she taught in English, and as I tried to strike up a conversation with her, her English just seemed to get worse and worse. Her accent wasn't quite Italian, and it wasn't quite German, nor could you say it was Spanish or French. I couldn't figure this lady out really, even though her blond hair gave her away as something of the Teutonic variety.

I asked her if it would be better that we spoke in Italian, as I figured maybe since she lived in town, her Italian would be better than her English. Just about anything would have been better than her English. So we switched gears into Italian, and I was started to find that her Italian was just as bad as her English. Finally, we switched into some broken Spanish (my

Spanish was rusty at this point) and again, I was amazed to find that I spoke better Spanish than she did!

It turns out that she spoke 8 languages! And none of them well! I asked where she was from and she said Germany, but that her German wasn't even all that good. I asked her what she spoke well, and she replied that English and Italian were her two best languages. She had apparently moved around a lot as a kid, and picked up a bit of everything as she moved.

I guess we can all be like that at times- Jack-of-all-trades, master of none. But it is an expectation in our culture that we multi task- that we keep as many plates spinning as we possibly can without letting any of them fall. And there are plenty of people who are waiting for our plates to fall! The expectation is that we are supposed to be good at everything we do- be good soccer moms and executives- be good dads and football coaches- be members of the church and work and community- have a thousand friends who we write thousands of Christmas cards to. It can be maddening I tell ya!

But I often think of that professor in Rome- she couldn't really speak any language well, and our conversation turned into a mishmash of English, Spanish, and Italian. If we lose our focus, we will certainly be destroyed, simply because we can't keep all those plates spinning at once.

I once had a similar experience- I once took 22 credit hours one semester in college- studying 3 languages (Latin, Greek, and Spanish) in addition to all the philosophy credits I was expected to take. I didn't learn any of those languages well, and I would have to say that by the end of the semester it was even hard to get my English straight! (I remember my friend jabbing me with a friendly insult, and all I could do was stare at him, because no coherent English words were going to come out.)

If we lose our focus and diversify our life so much that we spread ourselves thin, all we are going to be able to do is to stare at someone when they need a response. The same is true in our professional occupation as well- McDonald's used to have good hamburgers, until they spread out into salads and chicken and cookies and all the other things that they do. If they focused on being the number one hamburger maker, maybe it wouldn't turn my stomach so bad when someone suggests it as a nice pit stop on a trip.

We can simply keep pulling the lever and hope for a jackpot- the reason slot machines work is because it is hard to take three diverse things and line them up!

A possible solution is that we need to streamline our lives a little- understand what is important to us so that we can be a good focused person, and help the people around us. That means saying "NO" sometimes; that means drawing and keeping our boundaries with people and with ourselves. It means cutting out the fat and not sticking too many "irons in the fire."

There are five areas of our life that we need to maintain- Spiritual, Intellectual, Physical, Professional, and Social. Those are the five necessary components to being a happy person, and yet we have to prioritise even those areas. Setting short term easily attainable goals in each of these areas, and cutting out the fat when necessary will make us a well-rounded person. Even then, there are times in which one of these will take president over the others. We have to make sure that we are maintaining a balance in all of our lives.

Think of it like food- when I get a plate of food I might have a piece of meat, a potato, and a vegetable. Rarely do I try and eat all three at once- I like to enjoy the individual flavour of each- to mix them takes away from the flavour of each part of the meal. In the end we have to know where to quit and when to say yes. I would recommend a book by Seth Godin called "The Dip."

If we stop trying to spin 10 plates, it may be easier to spin 5- now we just have to decide which plates to stop from spinning.

More Important Than the Bible: Opinion and Truth

Do you remember those pesky magic eye puzzles that were all the rage ten or fifteen years ago? About the same time as we were trying to find that stupid Waldo guy (who apparently liked to hang out in large crowds... I can relate) every single mall had a kiosk where they sold these stupid magic eye puzzles.

To the naked eye, it looked like a Jackson Pollock painting- a hodgepodge (love that word) of colours sort of splattered onto a poster. Apparently, if you stared at this thing long enough, crossed your eyes, stood on your head, and had a few drinks, the image would change and you would see a farm-scape or a sail boat, or Waldo, in 3D appear before your very eyes. It just so happened that the next kiosk over sold little bottles of Advil and eye drops, because not only did you have a headache from staring at these stupid posters, but your eyes dried out because you had to hold them open for so long trying to figure out if it was a monkey or a baseball bat that magically appeared out of the mixture of colours and textures. These stupid things were just as popular back then as hyper-colour t-shirts. (Yea... remember those? If you touched them they changed colour because of the heat in your hand. Until you washed them once. I am sure those shirts poisoned us all somehow. Maybe that is how we could see that magic eye puzzle- the hyper colour t-shirts were making us hallucinate.)

I have to admit trying out these magic eye puzzles myself the first time. I walked by the kiosk and saw people just staring into the collection of various eye puzzles, and decided to join the herd. 3 hours later, I think I saw a camel in a space suit pop out in 3D.

There were always three types of people at these kiosks- the people that would walk up and look into the magic eye puzzle and instantly yell out (as if any of us cared) "I SEE IT!! IT IS A SUNSET IN TOKYO IN JUNE!" Others, grumbling, also loud enough for people to hear, "I just can't see it, it is just a bunch of colours running together... I just can't see it... are you sure that's there?" The third type of person was the type that felt sorry for the second type of guy who couldn't see the dolphin jumping out of a bowl of spaghettio's and would help out assuring the incapable person- "It'll be alright- just relax- let your eyes cross- don't you see the dolphin? He's right over there!"

I think that the most entertaining feature of the magic eye puzzle was not the magic eye puzzle itself, but watching the people stare for minutes at a time into what looked like a child's finger painting.

I did eventually see the images pop out of the posters, and it was neat, but I wonder if there was anything there at all, or if I was just buying into the hype of the magic eye puzzle. Maybe there was something there and maybe there wasn't- was it my own perception, or was I borrowing the perception from my neighbor who gleefully "got it?"

Here is an interesting fact I heard recently- up to 90% (90%!!!!) of our perceptions are borrowed from other people.

I will let that sink in for just a minute.

It's like Homer Simpson once said- 42% of statistics are made up on the spot, but only 12% of people know that. Sometimes we trust in the perceptions of others more than we know.

So when it comes to a world view- a cosmology, as the philosophers like to coin it, a lot of our views come from what other people have told us. I think that is what Nietzsche was talking about when he was talking about his "will to power." The will to power is the ability to impose our own perception onto the people around us. It works- just watch the news. They are imposing their views on us all the time, and I am even tempted to believe it simply because it is easier to believe them than to do the research on my own. I don't have the time, the resources or the energy to do that.

Perception is a tricky thing. There are as many perceptions as there are people- if I am looking at this chair, and so are you, we may be seeing the chair differently- I may think it is red, and you may think it is violet. Perceptions, whether given or borrowed, are never 100% accurate. That is where communication comes in, in order that we may cut through what is mere opinion to the objective truth underneath. Life is constantly about that- it is a constant battle that I think a lot people really don't engage in too well because it is a lot of work. Rather, they would just prefer to accept the perceptions of others- culture, media, or what have you.

What is more important than the chair in our above example is not the chair necessarily, but our perception and our interpretation of the chair.

In a like manner, when we talk about theology, more specifically the Bible, it really isn't the Bible that is important these days, but it is MY personal interpretation of the Bible that is important. You can really interpret the Bible in any way you want- a great example that I like to use is the whole slavery issue in the history of the United States- the abolitionists used the Bible to go against slavery, while the south used it to support slavery.

So when it comes down to it these days, what is more important than the Bible, or the Koran, or the Torah,

A Cure For Heartburn
www.FatherWagner.com

or the Big Book in this culture, is our personal interpretation of the book- I can interpret those books to mean whatever I want them to mean- or whatever someone has told me to interpret them as. In order to interpret the Bible in the proper way we would need to go back to the original intention of the author (and the Spirit that inspired that author) and begin from there for a proper and true interpretation. Otherwise the snake handlers are just as justified to handle snakes as any other practice of the mainstream religions.

It is a fine line between figuring out the truth and separating it from mere opinion or perception. As I said, this is probably the work of our lives, because the intellect seeks the truth. I do not think that there is a simple answer to this problem, as it goes back to the radical individualism of our modern western culture. Truth is out there though, it is simply not a matter of perception, but finding the truth requires us in some sense to question the perceptions that we have, the perceptions that others have, and to find the truth that underlies it all. That doesn't mean that a generally accepted perception isn't necessarily true, but we should deeply question EVERYTHING in our search for what is true and what is merely opinion.

There are two philosophers that come to mind here that I think would be important to mention. The first is Francis Bacon, and the other is Martin Heidegger.

Both of these guys were advocates of what I am talking about- Bacon said that we have preconceived "idols" of the marketplace- accepted notions that were given to us by our upbringing and enculturation that we accept as truth. That doesn't mean that they aren't true, but that we need to toss them out every so often to test them to find which is true, and which is simply an "idol." Heidegger on the other hand advocates a similar plan- that is to "step into the clearing of being," in other words like a forest to step into a clearing that the sun (being) is unobstructed by the trees of perception and opinion.

Only when we step into the clearing of being, and get rid of the idols of the marketplace, can we begin to compare our own and others perceptions of things- including things like religious texts like the Bible, to the truth.

I remember my first day in philosophy class ten years ago- we studied Plato on the difference between mere opinion and truth. Its conclusion was that opinion can be true, but isn't necessarily true, and it is our task- really our deepest desire- to separate opinion from what is objectively true. That's about as hard sometimes as seeing those pesky pictures in the magic eye posters.

At the end of the day, finding truth is sort of like picking Waldo out of one of those "Where's Waldo" pictures. There are a lot of things that LOOK like

A Cure For Heartburn
www.FatherWagner.com

Waldo that are not, just like there are things that APPEAR true which are not. We can never be content with a look a like to the truth, just like we are not done with our search until we find Waldo, or see the 3D image in the magic eye poster.

(Part 1) My Junior Prom and My First Time Shaving, Oh and I Got Dumped too...

Oh my Junior Prom...   It would have made a great episode of the <u>Wonder Years</u>. When I think about it, I can almost hear Daniel Stern narrating the background.

Back in High School, there was this new girl who had just moved into town- let's call her Monica, of course, to protect the innocent. OK she really isn't that innocent... but I guess her identity should still be protected.

She had moved in from another state in the south, and she was cute as a button... OK she was really good looking... cute just doesn't suffice. So I buddied up with her in physics class, since she sat next to me, and I turned on the ol' Wagner charm. I was witty, funny, insightful... as much as a Junior in High School could be and eventually I got her to go out on a date with me. We went to see <u>Billy Madison</u>. I still cringe when I see that movie, although it does open with a guy in a penguin suit, so instantly I forget my woes.

Eventually, I asked Monica to the prom. 3 months before the prom. She said yes and I was sooooo happy. I about shot out of the car like a rocket! I bought her flowers and gifts and all sorts of stuff- I really, really liked her a lot. I think it embarrassed her a little... or a lot.

The night came for the prom, and with my youthful features I decided to shave for the first time- cutting a big gash in my faced with the razor, just below my right eye. There was no reason to be shaving, let alone shaving under my eye, but I saw the flap of skin come down, and the blood began to flow. It wouldn't have been so bad had I not already been dressed in my tux (complete with tails by the way) (I had a cane too... I just needed a top hat and a monocle to make the look complete,) and the limo had just pulled up. Luckily, I had plenty of band-aids and gauze on hand. (My Mom is a nurse.)

We got to my friend's house, and he had a brilliant idea to help me with my bleeding problem- so he ran into his house, grabbed a green bottle of rubbing alcohol, and told me to put some on the gauze and put it in the wound.

A cry went through the land. Birds flew away, dogs howled in the distance, and somewhere a monkey fell out of a tree.

By the way, not only does rubbing alcohol sting, it makes things bleed faster. That is just an FYI.

Anyway, we picked Monica up at her house, and she

came out looking like... well... I guess I should be nice. She looked... is there a nice way to say this? She looked like... a "professional?" You know what I mean? I was embarrassed in front of my three other friends and their dates.

Then she got into the limo, and said, for all to hear- "by the way, my boyfriend told me that if you touch me, he is going to beat you up."

"Huh," I thought," I thought I was your boyfriend." I guess I was mistaken. That may have hurt a little. She didn't even think my shaving scar was cool.

I really had it for this girl- I got a tux with tails and a limo, and we went to the most expensive restaurant in town, called The Refectory. We walked in, and sat down, and she ordered the most expensive thing on the menu. Rabbit I believe. Took a single bite and finished eating.

"Huh," thought I. I simply said, "If you aren't going to eat it, then I will." Good thing I like rabbit. Tastes like chicken. (By the way, why is rabbit so expensive? It's not like they have a problem making more.) (Rabbit is a renewable resource.)

We went to the dance. I did cut a rug, and even boogied a little. Sometimes with Monica. Sometimes without. I dance like a brick with arms. That is, I never move my feet, just my arms. I do "raise the roof" sometimes, I have to admit.

At the end of the night, we decided to go bowling- I had to hold her pager because there was no room in her "professional" dress to hold it, and for some strange reason, she got paged a half dozen times at 2 AM. It was an "emergency" and she had to go. I was ready for her to go anyway.

So I took her home and she asked me if I was upset at her. I said no. I was just done. Maybe a little hurt. So I ended the evening back and my friend's house, where I got to sit on the couch while the other guys hung out with their dates. AWKWARD!

(Part 2) Lust, Luv, and Love

See there are three basic aspects to the human person when it comes to relationships with other people. There are two ways in which we are made in the image and likeness of God- first is that we have free will (or at least we are designed to have free will) and the second is that we can enter into relationships with people- that is we have the ability to know someone and do what is good and right for them. These two things, freedom and relationships culminate in one word: Love. This makes us in the image and likeness of God.

Half the movies out there are romantic comedies. They are so formulaic it is almost sickening- boy meets girl, boy loses girl, boy does something to win girl back. Yet, every time a new version of <u>Pretty Woman</u> comes out, or <u>Hope Floats</u>, or whatever, people go in droves to see it- even though the actors and setting are different, the basic plot is almost always the same. I am not making fun of that genre, but it tells us something about who we are as people- we have a need and a desire to love and to be loved, and if we can't have it for ourselves, we are happy to live it vicariously through someone else.

How about music? Turn on the pop channels- or country- heck even rap- they are, to some extent, almost inundated with love songs (and a great deal of break up songs) (am I the only one who notices that?) Nobody is singing about puppies or lollipops any more... not without some hidden meaning.

In our culture "love" is a bankrupted word. We use it for anything- to quote Steve Carell's character in Anchorman, "I love lamp."

I suspect that if you asked the 11th grade Josh Wagner how he felt about Monica back then, he would have said that he was in love with her. That is why it hurt so bad when so totally ripped out my heart, threw it on the ground and stomped on it... OH AND ANOTHER THING.... oh ... sorry. Ahem...

I doubt I was in love with her- there are a lot of things that mask themselves as love- love itself is so dynamic that the Greeks needed three words for it! Philos (Friendship) Eros (Romance) and Agape- disinterested, self- giving love.

Lust (Oh no!)

I suspect that a lot of people confuse lust and love- there is no such thing as love at first sight folks- that is lust. This uncontrollable urge to be drawn to someone or even something- that sort of sentiment that drives us crazy... that is lust. If it is irrational, it is lust. Now lust I suspect serves a good purpose, or it wouldn't be part of who we are as people. Maybe half the people reading this wouldn't be here if it weren't for lust! I guess I should draw a distinction- lust is an irrational and seemingly uncontrollable attraction- not to be confused (necessarily) with finding someone attractive. Romeo and Juliet is not a story about love, as we all might think it is, but a story about lust. Most of those romantic comedies I mentioned before are the same way. The movie ends, and the boy and girl are together, finally, and they live happily ever after... what we don't get to see is ten years down the line when he is fat and bald, and she has gained 40 lbs. That is when you get to see love.

Luv-

This is a sort of in between stage. Luv isn't bad either. As a friend of mine once said, this is puppy love. We all need that- those sort of "butterflies in my stomach" feeling that we get when we first begin to fall in love with someone, and all the dopamine shoots off in their head every time a couple meets. That is also a good thing- half of people get married because of this feeling- probably the other half of us that are reading this are here because of Luv. I hope we all get to experience this sometime in our lives- I think it is what Sonny and Cher were singing about when they said: "I Got You Babe." It is that feeling that lets you see past some of the bad, and get to the core of the good. It is that Luv, which initially attracts us to the other person- it, is fun and free- this kind of Luv is easy to do, and it makes us believe that we can make it through any trial. Nothing wrong with any of those feelings- but they are just that still- feelings. They are a nice mixture though of reason and emotions- all good things. It isn't wild and out of control like lust, but it isn't quite as deep and meaningful as Love. It also comes and goes as a feeling- nobody is in Luv forever... but people fall in and out of "Luv" all the time. Sometimes with the same people. I think that is what happens when people have a rocky time in marriage- they just may not be as in "Luv" as they were before. It is certainly possible to re-kindle that feeling. It hurts to "fall out of Luv" with someone because that feeling is so good to have, and it is something that we want and need. It is pleasant to say the least. Luv can make us cling to another person because we are afraid of how we might feel without them.

Love

True Love is a toughy I think. It is not something you fall in or out of- it is a choice that we make. Loving is simply willing the good of another- it is a totally rational thing. Certainly emotion, and how we feel about someone can make it easier to love someone-but Love should never be based on emotion. As I always like to say, Love is a choice, not a feeling. I think we have lost sight of that these days- maybe the human race has never gotten it right. Love is what Christ preaches in the Bible and shows us on the cross. St. Paul has it right when he says in Corinthians:

"Love is patient, Love is kind. It does not envy, it does not boast, it is not proud. It is not rude, it is not self-seeking, it is not easily angered, it keeps no record of wrongs. Love does not delight in evil but rejoices with the truth. It always protects, always trusts, always hopes, always preserves."
-- 1 Corinthians 13:4-7

Love, in and of itself is disinterested and detached- it is never self-centered or self seeking, rather it seeks the good- the fulfilment of the highest potential that a person is capable of receiving and becoming. Love never counts the cost- it simply is a choice for the good.

As I mentioned before we are made in the image and likeness of God, which means we can freely enter into relationships- in other words we are made in the image and likeness of God because we have the ability, unlike any other creature in heaven and on earth, to love. Love is not a one-time choice- it is a choice that we must make over and over again.

We simply cannot love what we do not know, so Love is based on knowledge- when we know someone, and ourselves, we will know what good needs to be done so that they may be what God has created us to be.

Luv isn't a bad thing- it is the beginning stages that hopefully will turn and deepen into Love- it is Love's prerequisite as well.

Love therefore, must be synonymous with freedom. Sometimes to love someone we have to let them go because it is the best thing- sometimes to love we have to walk away from a situation that isn't the healthiest for us, even if it is hard or unpleasant to do so. Sometimes it means taking a risk instead of doing what is easy or safe to do. Love always involves a risk, as to do the good for others, we must sometimes sacrifice our own pleasure or luxury in order that a person might find the good they need in their lives.

Luv makes us clingy; Love lets us be free. That is when you truly know people are in love- when they continually make the choice to "be there," without compulsion or fear- if we love someone we must always give them the option of walking away from us if it is the best thing for them at the time. That can stink really... maybe there are times when we need to walk away too.

A Cure For Heartburn
www.FatherWagner.com

Love doesn't always have to be about sacrifice- Love can also mean making the choice to receive the gift of Love that someone is giving to us. That can be hard- maybe we don't feel like we have the right or the ability to be loved. Maybe we spend all day loving others, and never love ourselves, or let ourselves be loved. Pretty soon the "Love Tank" is going to be on empty, and no one is going to be able to be loved.

Love is specifically what makes us human- the choice, despite how we might be feeling, to do the right thing for ourselves and the people in our lives. That means constant growth and communication- forgiveness of others and ourselves when we fail to love, as we should.

Love is a tough choice to make sometimes, but it is always, ALWAYS a fulfilling choice to make.

Here are some statements on Love that I like to make:

Love is a choice not a feeling
Love is willing the good of another
Love is an action, not an emotion
Love is based on freedom
Love is disinterested and detached- it is never self seeking
Love is the gift of self
You can't love what you don't know

Neither this chapter, nor that above list is exhaustive

of the concept of Love. I am not sure anyone can exhaust this particular topic! To do that would be to define the entirety of the human race, God, and the entire world!

A Cure For Heartburn

5 Part Series: Getting Your Ducks in a Row

Introduction: Getting your Ducks in a Row

About a year ago, it was time for my Mom to move out of the house that I had gone to High School in, and which she had lived for the previous 14 years. There were a lot of memories in that house- it is the house where my Father passed away- it is the house that I "left home" from, and that I often returned to, to visit my parents, and our dog, Snuggles. I did not name the dog- we adopted her. Admittedly, she was a cock-a-poo, so while Snuggles actually kind of fit her, I am pretty sure she hated that name. I would have named her Bone Crusher, or Megatron, after one of the Transformers if I had my druthers. But I never have my druthers. I am druther free. No druthers for me.

As we were in the process of moving Mom out of her house, where she was by herself and only using about 20% of it, and into her condo, Mom had a phrase that she liked to use. Nothing could go on in life, until she got her "ducks in a row." There were many ducks to get into a row when we were moving Mom- I know. I helped move all those damned ducks with my brothers. Actually, the ducks in a row thing become something of a joke between all of us and we often

A Cure For Heartburn
www.FatherWagner.com

laughed about it.

When the moving guys came to move the big stuff
that would have otherwise given my brothers and me
back trouble and hernias, I remember looking out the
window at the moving truck, and not thinking much
of it. Then I saw it. There was a giant duck on the
side.

I pointed this out to my family, and we all shared a
chuckle. Mom said she didn't hire them because of
the ducks. I am beginning to wonder.

At any rate, "ducks in a row" is a phrase that my
spiritual director likes to use as well. He says in that
in our lives we have 5 basic psychological needs- "five
ducks" - that we have to keep in line if we want to live
a happy and sane life. The problem with these
psychological and emotional ducks is the same
problem with real ducks: they tend to wonder around
and get out of line. There is nothing worse, I imagine,
than trying to wrangle up a bunch of stray ducks. It
is probably a constant struggle if you yourself are not
a duck.

In short, we are trying to get our ducks in a row all
the time, or we should be. I think a lot of people don't
try to keep their ducks in a row by good healthy
means, but through things like trying to get the ducks
drunk, or to feed them until they can't move, or by
spending lots of money on things they don't need.

A Cure For Heartburn
www.FatherWagner.com

There is a lot of ways to try and cage the "ducks" rather than keeping them in line- but the catch in our lives is that not only do we have to keep our ducks in a row, we also have to do it in freedom- not by some artificial means.

So what are these 5 ducks that my Spiritual Director told me about?
Self- Worth
Ability to love and be loved
Ability to defend myself
Ability to deal with my own inner confusion
Ability to accept the consequences of my actions

I think these are pretty good "ducks," and a lot of the spiritual direction that I get from him concerns these ducks.

The First Duck: Understanding your Self-Worth

My spiritual director is a great Jesuit who I got to know in Rome years ago when he was the director of spiritual formation at the North American College. When I arrived in Rome, tired, smelly from the flight, and covered in ketchup (that is another story) they shoved us into the refectory for our first Italian meal. My now spiritual director was at my table, and was the first people I ate with in that city. I remember him making bruschetta (pronounced Bru-sk-ett-a) out of the bread on the table when he toasted it and poured cheese and olive oil on it. He was a good salad maker as I recall as well. Beyond that, I really never knew him until I got a friend's ordination a few years ago in Michigan, and he offered to be my Spiritual Director. He has stuck with me in these last years in thick and thin- he has been a real blessing to me, and I am sure others who have struggled through the years.

The first of the five ducks, or psychological needs that we have to wrangle up, is that of self worth. Man have I struggled with that. Where do we get our self worth? How do we find it? What are the sorts of things that prevent us from realizing our self worth?

Primarily, as I have mentioned in the previous

chapter, we are made in the image and likeness of God, which has two implications by nature. One is that we have free will, or we should have it, and second is that we are capable of entering into relationship with other people. Free will and the ability to enter into relationship culminate in love. Love, as my director tells me, is willing the good of another. I always say that love is a choice, not a feeling, so even if it hurts, we have to do what is the greatest good for our communities, our neighbors, and ourselves.

That being made in the image and likeness of God is what primarily gives us our self worth. No other creature, not dogs or angels, can claim to be made in God's image and likeness. They cannot express free will, or enter into relationships in love the way that we can.

The problem is that we have a hard time perceiving that we are made in that image and likeness. The primary cause of that: Sin.

Sin primarily detracts from the beauty and worth of every person, not because it destroys the fact that we are in the image and likeness of God, but because it tarnishes it like a mirror can get tarnished, making it difficult to see our reflection of God's divine nature. When we sin, in any of the stages, our instant reaction is like the of Adam and Eve's- we see that we are naked, and we are ashamed of ourselves, heck, we even become ashamed of the fact that we are not living up to the image and likeness of God in which we were created. That leads us to do what they did- they cover themselves- they cover their nature.

So it is sin that detracts from us seeing our self worth- that dignity that we have been made in God's image and likeness- each and every person. From the greatest saint, to the greatest murderer, nothing can take that image and likeness to God away from us, but sin can make it harder for us to see.

So we constantly have to rediscover our self worth- we really do need to have this duck in a row if we are going to get the others in line. We want to know we are worthwhile, and we will, without a doubt, seek some kind of validation of that self worth, or we will try to cover it like Adam and Eve, and we will be ashamed of something that is so beautifully created by God.

Some of the ways that we try and find validation is through relationships. That is OK if the relationship is healthy. Often though we seek people that we relate to, or are similar to, in order that we might validate ourselves in them. Sometimes that means multiple marriages, sexual partners, remaining in abusive situations, or any number of things. There are people that constantly seek the validation that only God can give to them.

There are ways of covering it up too. People who are ashamed of themselves cannot face or accept that they are worthwhile and try to cover their nature with booze, or drugs, or shopping, eating, jobs, uniforms, or any number of potential addictions that are out there. We can even be addicted to people or ideologies!

In the end if we truly want to find our self worth, we have to peek into ourselves- take the good with the bad, and see that underneath it all, we still have that beauty and that dignity of being made in the image and likeness of God, despite the fact that we are a bit tarnished at times by our choices to turn away from the inherent dignity that is in each person.

The other way to find self worth requires a bit of spirituality I think. We need to see ourselves as God sees us. He doesn't require us to be handsome or smart or funny or have a great job or a great car or any number of things that give us validation in our culture. Rather, he loves just because we exist. Unconditionally. Whether we love Him back or not. That is the ultimate validation of our self worth.

Once we begin to realize that we have self worth, it directs us toward putting our second duck in a row- the need to love and to be loved.

The Second Duck: The Need to Love and to Be Loved

A few years ago, of my favorite movies came to the big screen: <u>Moulin Rouge</u>. Nicole Kidman, Ewan McGregor, and even that short guy that plays the creepy clown in <u>Spawn</u> was in it. Man, as if clowns weren't creepy enough, he had to go and play an even creepier clown in that <u>Spawn</u> movie. Frankly, I just find John Leguizamo creepy, whether he is dressed as a clown or not.

For those of you who haven't seen the movie, <u>Moulin Rouge</u> is about a burlesque house in Paris, France, near Mon Martres. Mon Martres was famous, and still is, for many things; among the most notable are the artists. Like many houses of ill repute, Moulin Rouge enjoyed a considerable amount of success for its time, which was about the turn of the 20th century. The movie itself was about a particularly famous actress falling in love with a penniless writer. There was a lot of singing involved, particularly of songs by Sting.

Anyway, I loved the movie, and around the time Moulin Rouge (the movie) was reaching the heights of its own popularity, I was taking a trip to France to see Paris. We saw all the sites in that fair city, including

A Cure For Heartburn
www.FatherWagner.com

the top of Mon Martres, and the glorious Sacre Coeur church that sits on top of it. We ate a nice lunch, and saw some of the artists that hung around doing portraits of people.

I was with my friend; lets call him Mitch (to protect the innocent). Mitch had been having a tough week as they had lost his luggage in our trip from Rome to Paris. All he had to wear was the clothes that he travelled in. The airline was nice enough to give him a toothbrush though.

So Mitch and I finished lunch and looked into the guidebook for the next thing to see. It turns out that St. Ignatius of Loyola had founded the Society of Jesus on that very mountain, so we strolled down Mon Martres, faithfully following our guide book to the street where the church was built. Since we both attended a Jesuit school in Rome, we figured that we had to pay our respects. It was about 3:00 in the afternoon so it was locked. (I suspect everyone was taking their afternoon nap.)

Disappointed we looked into our guidebook for something else to do, and lo and behold, the Moulin Rouge was just down the street and around the corner! I told Mitch that we had to go since I was rather enamoured by the movie <u>Moulin Rouge</u>, and it would be silly to miss. He seemed hesitant. He never told me why but I was about to find out.

A Cure For Heartburn

Now, something should have told me this was a bad idea, but images of Nicole Kidman were dancing through my head. That something was that two older gentlemen, dressed as two older women, were standing at the end of the street waving at us. Their faces looked like melted candles. I pointed at them and said to Mitch, "hey look at those two." They waved back, and said hello to us. I thought it was funny. Mitch did not.

That didn't deter me though, as we took a left at the elderly cross dressers and went further down the mountain. My face was buried in the book trying to make sure we were going the right direction. We got to the bottom of the hill and turned right. Mitch immediately let out a rather loud, "oh no!" I looked up, and there it was. More neon than I had ever seen in my life: we were in the "red light" district of Paris.

Mitch was scared. I was frankly scared. I have never been in a more disturbing place in my life. It was all around us, like we had walked through the closet in the <u>Lion the Witch and the Wardrobe</u>, but instead of appearing in Narnia, we appeared in a much scarier place. Mitch told me that we should get out of here... I tried to act calm and I told him that there was a subway stop about a block ahead, conveniently placed right in front of the Moulin Rouge.

As we walked, there were people (fully clothed) standing in front of the various... "establishments"...

trying to get us into the door. I was trying to play it off as if it wasn't disturbing, but Mitch wasn't doing so well. I said to him, "Mitch, they aren't going to attack us!" At that very moment, one of the door people grabbed Mitch by the arm, dragging him toward the door, and said- "You come with me sweetie!"

Mitch let out a groan of terror. I started laughing. It was too much really.

So I fought off the door person, and we shuffled down what seemed to be the never-ending block toward the Moulin Rouge. I looked up, and there it was. No Nicole Kidman, no Ewan McGregor- no creepy John Leguizamo. Just a neon covered Red Windmill spinning in the afternoon sun. It was still a burlesque house. The guidebook seemed to leave that whole part off of its description.

Mitch was ready to go, as was I. The subway entrance was just a few feet away when I saw it- a candy stand. I walked over and bought some gummy bears. I got a bag full and then we got on the subway to wherever we ended up next. I came to find Mitch wasn't real happy with our adventure, but he eventually forgave me, as it was an honest mistake.

There was a constant theme that went through the entire movie of Moulin Rouge- the Penniless writer, played by Ewan McGregor, came to Paris, not only to write, but to fall in love. The constant theme throughout the movie was that there is nothing greater in this world, than to love and to be loved. That brings us to the second duck that my spiritual director told me about last week. It is absolutely on the money. Of course, once Ewan McGregor expresses publicly his love for Nicole Kidman's character, she dies of tuberculosis. I am sorry if I spoiled the ending for you... you have had 7 years to watch it.

This is a fundamental human need that we have though- to love and to be loved. Some people have a hard time with some aspects of this "duck" for various reasons.

There are some people that are easy to love. Some people that when we see them, it brightens our day, and it makes us feel good. There are others, however, that are not so easy to love- sometimes it is a friend, or a co-worker, or a member of the family. Love is not always an easy thing to do, but Love is what we are made for. As I have said in other posts, we are made in the image and likeness of God, which means that we have free will, and second, we have the ability to enter into relationships. These culminate in Love- Love is the choice of willing the good of another person.

Sometimes willing the good of another person means that we have to give them up. Sometimes it means doing something, or not doing something, that we might not want to do in order that we do what is best for our neighbor. Love is very, very difficult, but we have a need to love because it takes us out of ourselves, and is the basis for every relationship that we have, from friendship to family or even co-workers. Love at least should be the basis for those relationships. Love turns us away from ourselves, and improves the other person by letting them become the best that they can be. Love hurts sometimes too- real love does, because it involved risk and sacrifice. Risk that our gift of self may be rejected or mis-understood, and sacrifice, which is at the core of loving others- doing what is right for them and best for them, even if it is tough to do.

Believe it or not though, I believe that loving others is the easier of the two. Accepting Love is really hard for some people to do, because they don't think they are worthy, or they have never really been loved. Accepting Love means admitting that you need love- it also involves risk- the risk of letting someone know you, and exposing what is in the deepest parts of your heart. See, you can't love what you don't know, so often we reject Love to protect those things in our hearts that we think are unlovable.

This is what shame is- our whole culture is based around shame for a good part- shame is the belief that there is something unlovable about me- something we are embarrassed to show. People who are abused often feel this- not only do they not let other people love them, but they have a hard time loving themselves. Being loved involves even more of a risk than loving someone else, simply because in order to be loved you have to be open and honest with yourself and others in order for them to love you.

That is where God comes into the picture. He loves us unconditionally. There is nothing we can do to lose that love, and nothing we need do to earn it. God knows us better than we know ourselves, and always does what is best for us. Sometimes that means saying no to us as well. The key and the goal is to begin to see ourselves as God sees us- to let Him love us, so that we might imitate that toward ourselves and others.

There is no amount of shame that God cannot love away if we let Him. Then we ourselves can be loved, and in turn, go out and love others- finding out what they need and their greatest good and willing that. This fulfils who we are as human beings, allowing us to freely enter into a loving relationship with God, ourselves, and other human beings.

The Third Duck: The Need to Learn to Defend Yourself

Back in the 80's I remember sitting through horrible episodes of Saturday Night Live (ok they weren't as bad as some of them now) just to watch American Gladiators. I am not sure why the show ever went off the air, other than the fact that they messed with some of the more popular games, eliminating some of them all together, or replacing them with goofy substitutes that they thought would liven things up. I mean, who liked that stupid swinging one anyway? That was just dumb if you ask me.

It was a great concept- average Americans- Americans just like you or me taking on buff, steroid induced machines in some really physically challenging competitions. Well, some of them were physically challenging anyway. Like the "Eliminator," at the end of every show, or the one where they had to out-clime one of those buff Gladiators on a climbing wall. It was great competition as the Gladiator, who was always in much better shape than the opponent scaled the wall like Spider-man to pull down his contender.

There were games though that required almost no physical prowess whatsoever. I can't remember the name of it, but one of the games gave the Gladiator a

A Cure For Heartburn
www.FatherWagner.com

high-powered gun that shot tennis balls at the contender. The contender had to hit a target just above the Gladiator's head to win, using only tennis balls thrown by his arm. (OK he had some weapons of his own, but they never seemed to have great aim.) The Gladiator would just sit up there and fire tennis balls at Mach 5 at the contender's head. Now that is good TV.

Sadly, the original Gladiators Zap, Laser, Gemini, Mitch, and Sneezy, (I may have some of those names wrong) got cancelled and had to go back to working at Pay-less, as the most buff shoe salesmen ever. They faded into obscurity, only to be seen in re-runs.

Now they are bringing back the Gladiators, and the world will be a better place. Once again we get to see average American's get the crap beat out of them by over juiced men and women... I hope congress doesn't ask THEM about steroid use...

Still, you have to give those average athletes credit... I would never want to go against a person who calls themselves Viper or Ice. They often stood up against these big people and defended themselves well. My favorite event by far was the pugel-sticks, where they stood up on big pedestals with giant cue-tips and attacked each other. It was great.

Nobody stood there and took it though- they defended themselves, even if unsuccessfully, they still had to learn somehow along the line how to defend themselves. This is the third "duck" in the series of 5 ducks that I mentioned in a previous post.

One of our basic human needs is to learn how to defend ourselves. That can be hard to do- there are a lot of people that get into situations that prevent them from learning how to do this- to defend themselves physically, emotionally, or psychologically. It seems that they are going up against someone much more scary than any Gladiator could ever be- be it a parent, a spouse, a family member, or even a boss.

Some people think that in order for people to love them, or in order to love someone (the second "duck") that means that they have to let someone roll over them. That is not the case- each one of us needs to learn how to defend ourselves, in order that we might love others and ourselves. Being rolled over is not a loving thing to do for anyone.

Some people learn how to defend themselves inappropriately too. Some people turn to addictions to insulate themselves from their own emotions or fears. Drugs, alcohol, shopping, sex, food or whatever you want to put in that list (because you can be addicted to just about anything or anyone) is a quick and easy alternative to actually standing up to what we fear and defending ourselves in a healthy and appropriate way. In the end, those quick fixes that we use for self-defence end up isolating us from others and ourselves, they prevent us from loving or being loved, they add to our confusion, and diminish our self worth.

Another unhealthy way to defend ourselves is to try and control the situation- to roll over other people so that they cannot hurt us, or to try and manipulate situations so that we are always "King of the Mountain." Ultimately to roll over other people to defend ourselves is also self defeating for the same reason that addictions are. Basically, you begin to isolate yourself from other people as they come to fear you and your attitude and reactions to things.

Defending ourselves does not mean to isolate with addictions, or to try and control every single situation by rolling over people. In the end, it is more damaging to do either, and you will end up alone, fearful, and angry at the world. I have seen it happen in people's lives.

How do we properly defend ourselves? I believe the key is in setting healthy boundaries and then keeping them.

If we have someone in our lives that is toxic or dangerous to us, we have a right to set our own boundaries with that person. That doesn't mean imposing boundaries on them (that probably wouldn't work anyway) but it means that if we have a toxic person in our lives, we choose when to see them or not, the setting and the circumstance.

That means that defending ourselves is to not put ourselves into a situation that we will get hurt by. It means knowing ourselves well enough to set boundaries that are healthy, not exclusive, and it also means uttering the most difficult word: "No."

Setting boundaries means saying no to some things. Loving someone doesn't mean you always say yes to every desire that they have. Loving someone sometimes means you have to say no- it sometimes means that setting a boundary means that for their own good you have to put some distance between them and you. It doesn't mean that you don't love them, but what it means is that you love them enough to protect both yourself and them.

You don't even necessarily have to tell difficult people about your boundaries- it is you that has to keep them, not the other person. That may mean removing yourself from a dangerous or abusive situation. That may require you to ask for help in order to preserve yourself.

Really defending yourself and loving yourself aren't too different. It would be silly for that contender in American Gladiators to just stand there and take a beating from someone twice his size. We, like that contender, have a right to healthy self preservation- to say no- and to make sure that we are in an environment that is happy and healthy.

The Fourth Duck: Understanding and Dealing with Your Own Inner Confusion

Last year, during a cold snap in February, the roads were covered with salt, which meant my car, Lucy, was also covered in salt. Lucy is the greatest car I will ever own by the way... she is a red Pontiac G6 hard top convertible. It brings a tear to my eye when I think about her, she is so beautiful.

So on my way home from a friend's house late one night I was concerned for Lucy and the many layers of salt she had on her, and before accruing a new layer, I figured I would give her a quick run through the car wash.

I understand the absurdity of the idea of washing my car in below freezing temperatures, with salt coating the roads, and having to avoid the army of salt trucks I saw on the way home, but for some reason it seemed like a good idea. So I went to one of those "touchless" car wash, put my credit card in, the door opened and I pulled in, business as usual. The car wash ended and I am sure Lucy looked nice and clean. When it came time to leave, the garage door in front of me wouldn't open, and the one I came through was closed... so basically, I was trapped. I got out and pushed the emergency release button, and the door was still shut.

A Cure For Heartburn
www.FatherWagner.com

Frozen solid!

I was trapped...I was trapped!!! there was no door to the outside for humans either, and since I have not experienced the resurrection, and I am not David Copperfield (the fictional character nor the magician) I could not walk through the walls, and I felt a certain sense of dread come over me... Plus, inside the touchless car wash there is always water shooting from all directions, so to get out of my car was like walking through an obstacle course of water. At one point I was standing there thinking about what to do for a minute, when I realized that one of the streams of water was hitting the upper part of my right leg which I didn't feel for about 30 seconds, as the water was also warm... I don't have to tell you what that looked like... or felt like, as the water was very warm. Plus there was steam everywhere, which fogged up my glasses. I was in a bad position. I did begin to laugh at this point, and realized how funny the situation was. THEN I moved out of the way of the stream of water. HA!!! There was also no phone number posted to call, plus it was 10:30 at night. Anyway, I walked over to the other adjoining car wash chamber (great descriptive word there) (reminds me of the carbon freezing chamber from Star Wars), and I hit the release button for the garage door and that one opened. Instantly the steam increased 3 fold as it contacted the Arctic air outside; I must have looked like an alien emerging from the belly of the space ship.

Too bad nobody was there to see it. So it was cold, wet, and steamy, and my pant leg was drenched, but I had my sweet freedom. Except Lucy herself was still trapped. I called a number that I finally found and left a message for "Greg." Greg never got back to me, so I went back into the car wash, backed Lucy up to the back door, went around and bought another car wash, which opened up the back door and I backed her out into the cold, again in the midst of all is steam, Lucy emerged. Great story huh?

There were moments while I was trapped in that steamy mixture of cold air and hot water that I just didn't know what I was going to do. I was terrified at moments that I was going to have to spend the night in the middle of the car wash. Did I call 911? If I did, was it enough of an emergency and would I get in trouble? Worse yet, would the cops get there and just laugh at me? Talk about inner confusion! I was at my wits end! There were seemingly a thousand options that I could have pursued in securing my freedom, and none of them seemed adequate. Plus, once one door opened (literally!) all the other ones in front of me were still closed.

I think this is a great analogy to how a lot of people view life. They are in situations which baffle them-really it isn't the situation that baffles them; rather it is their own interior confusion that makes life-situations baffling to most people.

All of us deal to some extent with inner confusion. A lot of us like to avoid it because it makes us feel uncomfortable in our own skin. We are sort of like that car wash in some ways- like the water that was squirting in all directions, clouding up the cold air with steam, so we are often a flurry of emotions, thoughts, fears, rationalizations, and any number of things that "fog up" our interior "lenses," and prevent us from understanding who we really are, and what we need to do.

Dealing with this confusion is a basic human need. All of us get stuck in the car wash from time to time. Maybe we can relate to my little foible in the car wash last year- we know we are stuck in the steam and the sprays of water, closed behind doors that won't open due to our choices or circumstances, and we are too embarrassed or afraid to ask for help. I was afraid to call the police to get help because I figured they would laugh at me. Maybe some of us are ashamed about our own inner confusion and rather than seek help and be ridiculed or hurt, we prefer to spend the night in the chaos of our own "inner car wash."

Eventually, I took the time that night to think my way out of the car wash, and if we take the time, calm down, and really begin to look at our inner confusion,

A Cure For Heartburn
www.FatherWagner.com

both the causes and the effects, we may just figure out a way to free ourselves from the bondage of our own inner confusion. That takes work- it also invariably requires another person, or people to help us.

The first requirement is a relationship with a Higher Power. God made us; he can help us to figure out what is going on inside of us. He can calm us and give us a new perspective on our own inner confusion. Really we are wonderfully designed, and what seems like chaos to us is actually working properly. Going back to our car wash, the streams of water, the steam, and all the other elements of the confusion car wash told me that everything was working properly! It just seemed confusing to me! Once I figured out the glitch, I was free in a matter of minutes. Often what seems confusion to us is confusing because of a matter of perspective. God has the ultimate perspective on how we are supposed to work. Unlike "Greg" at the car wash, when we call on him he will come and help us fix the problem. We have to call Him first though.

Second, we need a community of support. Maybe that is family, maybe it isn't. Maybe it is friends or a support group. The first step to managing the seemingly unmanageable inner confusion we all face is admitting that we might have a problem, or a glitch in the mechanism. Once we do that we can go to people that can help us.

A Cure For Heartburn
www.FatherWagner.com

You can't see your own face without a mirror. We need someone outside of ourselves to be vulnerable to- both human and divine, that can help us sort out our inner confusion. This is an ongoing process if we want to be happy and free.

Of course, there are inappropriate ways to deal with inner confusion as well- avoidance behaviors that try and suppress the inner confusion we all face- Drugs, alcohol, bad relationships, or any number of things. These things not only are ineffective against suppressing our inner confusion, they make it worse.

In the end of the day, we simply need to make sure that we are rigorously honest with ourselves, our friends who we trust, and with God. We need to be humble enough to make that call when we need to when we are stuck in some situation, even when fear is telling us not to, or we are afraid of being hurt or made fun of. Only then can we begin to sort out that inner confusion which at one point or another, plagues us all.

A Cure For Heartburn
www.FatherWagner.com

The Fifth Duck: The Necessity of Dealing With the Consequences of Our Actions

Recently, that is, in the last few years, Staples, the paper and office supply company, had an advertising campaign where whenever someone pushed a big red "Easy Button," office supplies would magically drop from the ceiling. Whenever I see those commercials, and the big read button, I curl up into a ball and fall on the floor. Maybe I even cry a little bit. See, I have a thing for giant red buttons... PTSD (Post Traumatic Stress Disorder).

When I was about 12 years old, my Dad got transferred with IBM from our lush, expansive, peaceful, serene, and tranquil farm in Elida, Ohio, to the big bustling city of Dallas- Ft. Worth Texas, where IBM had its education center, and a hub for a big portion of its computer network.

Routinely, I would go to work with my Dad, and I would either spend hours playing with hole punches and staplers, or he would set me up at a computer where I could enter the world of computer role playing games, like Space Quest, or King's Quest, which were popular at the time. World of War Craft has nothing on King's Quest III, if you ask me.

One of these times, we were in the big mainframe room at one of the centers in Irving, Texas, where the IBM education center was. This room was expansive- so much so that if you threw a baseball, I doubt you could get it from one side of the room to the other. OK, I can't throw a baseball from home plate to first base, but you get the point!

This room was filled with huge mainframes, tape machines, terminals, and always had these gigantic air conditioners on keeping the whole place nice and cool. My dad found me a workstation and I began to solve the puzzle, which was <u>King's Quest IV</u>. I didn't like that one because you had to be a girl, unlike the previous couple of <u>King's Quests</u>, but I was content to play it anyway.

I got into the game, and began to realize that I needed to go to the bathroom. I waited for as long as I could, and the pain told me that we had a critical situation brewing. So I went over to my Dad and told him of my dilemma. He pointed out that the bathrooms were around the corner; outside of yonder door (pointing to yonder door). He told me that when I wanted to get back in, I had to push the button beside the door (which was probably some kind of door bell.)

I had to go to the bathroom so badly that my brain was floating, and some of the instructions that he had given me may have been misinterpreted... so I walked

A Cure For Heartburn
www.FatherWagner.com

over to the door and saw a button. All I could remember was to push the button. The button was large, and red, and had a plastic cover over it... kind of like the kind used to launch nukes in a movie.

I shrugged my shoulders and lifted the plastic cover, and pushed the big red button. All of sudden, the lights in the big room went off, as did all the computers, as well as the air conditioners, terminals, coffee pots, Ferris wheels etc. I had pushed the emergency cut off switch for the room. Not only that room, but also three of the buildings it was connected to.

All I remember is my Dad looking up in horror and asking me what I did.

I still had to go to the bathroom, so my Dad walked me down to the bathroom where I stayed for the next couple of hours. You would be surprised at how much flushing toilets can entertain you after awhile.

To this day when I see big red buttons, I feel nervous and anxious like I did that day. Shortly after, IBM issued a memo that family members were not to be in the building. Luckily, it was a Sunday, so it didn't disrupt commerce too much, although several guys had to be called in to reboot the buildings I had shut down. (Dad didn't get fired by the way, although he came awfully close.)

A Cure For Heartburn
www.FatherWagner.com

Whether we mean it or not, choose or not, intend it or not, we have to learn to live with the consequences of our own actions and choices. As creatures of free will, we are given the ability to make hundreds of big and small choices every day, one choice affecting the next. In our culture, it is very easy to try and escape the consequences of our own choices. That is a choice in itself, and eventually, we will have to face up, one way or another, to the choices that we have made.

It is impossible to escape consequences. We can't simply wait for things to work themselves out, as inactivity and indecision is itself a choice that we make. Living with the consequences of our actions can have both positive and negative effects. However, we are not ever bound and determined by choices we have made in the past. That is just because we made a choice that got us here, or into a particular situation, or set of circumstances or consequences, doesn't mean that we have to make those same decisions in the future.

Nor does it mean that we have to be determined by the consequences of other people's actions. What it means is that we must take responsibility for every choice we make, both good and bad, active and inactive, and work within the particular outcomes of each choice.

I didn't mean to push the wrong button that day, but I did. I had to accept and live with the potential consequences of that action. I could have either faced them, or run away from them, but either way they would have caught up with me.

We have a lot of means at our disposal for running from our consequences. Using these things to try and hide from consequences will only lead to more dire consequences in the future. The key here, as I mentioned above, is acceptance. Accepting what we have done in the past, understanding where it has brought us, and attempting to make better, more educated choices in the future.

There is a reason this is the last "duck," that we need to put in a row- simply because it is the duck that is the culmination of the other 4 "ducks" that came before it. If we understand our self worth, if we understand our need and fulfil our ability to love and be loved, if we defend ourselves, and deal with our own inner confusion, the consequences in every area of our life will be good, more or less. We will be able to handle any consequence that comes along because it is itself the consequence of putting our ducks in a row.

If we don't put those other 4 "ducks" in a row, we will have other consequences to deal with- being unhealthy- being scattered- never taking responsibility for our actions and trying to correct ourselves and stay on course.

This requires a lot of work to "keep our ducks in a row." Constant work, but the consequences of that work, of self examination, of proper love of self and neighbor, will itself lead us into good healthy decisions and consequences. So what we have to do is to accept where we have been, and use it as a jumping off point for where we would like to be.

Are your ducks in a row? Do you understand your worth? Do you love yourself and others? Can you defend yourself in a proper way? Where does your inner confusion lie? Do you accept the fact that you are where you are because of choices you have made? I know that personally, I have only been putting my ducks in a row in the last couple of years, and it requires a lot of constant work and vigilance. The consequences are worth it though.

"You are off route." (Accountability)

The title of this particular chapter comes from the naggy voice of my GPS system. She says that to me a lot. There were many good traits that I received from my parents, who are both very smart and talented people. My Mom always had a good sense of direction. So much so that my brother said you could blind fold her, drop her in the forest, and she would find her way back home and have dinner on the table before 5 o'clock. Dad on the other hand... did not have a good sense of direction. I remember once being lost with him on the road for a couple of hours. We were really lost. Guess which one I take after.

It is a good thing that we live in the modern age, or else I would still be driving around New Jersey right now. I have a terrible sense of direction. Hernando Cortez I am not... If you dropped me a in a forest, I would probably just sit down in the soft leaves and cry. I have done it before. In this time we have the great invention of the GPS- the Global Positioning System.

It is a neat invention really- it simply detects the multiple GPS satellites that are orbiting the earth, and somehow calculates your position based on the signal strength of those satellites relative to where you are standing on the globe. Then, you just punch in the address, and a little chime happens, letting you know the route has been created.

Even with a GPS though, I have managed to get lost... really lost.

I have a buddy... let's call him "Dave." Dave and I were searching for a good cup of coffee one night, so we decided to pull out his rusty, trusty, GPS, which had several entries for coffee shops in our area. Dave, by the way, has a bad sense of direction as well.

We selected one of the coffee shops on the list, something different from your typical Star Bucks, or Cup'O'Joe. We faithfully followed the GPS, turning here, turning there, and kept getting deeper and deeper into a neighborhood where finally the GPS dropped us off in front of a dimly lit, very nice house in a cal-du-sac. No signs. No aroma of freshly brewed coffee. Just darkness pierced every so often by the street lamps.

Dave and I looked at each other, understanding that the GPS had possibly lead us astray. We started laughing. I half considered just going up to the door of the house and asking them for a cup of coffee!

For the most part though, GPS systems are pretty reliable. Much like me, they may not give you the most direct route to get from point A to point B, but they usually get you there unscathed. Plus the nice thing is that the little voice comes over the GPS and gently (or in my GPS's case not so gently) and reminds us that we are off route. Then it is ever so kind as to show you how to get back on route.

It's too bad that we don't have built in GPS systems to let us know when we are off route. When it comes to me and my bad sense of direction I know I need something in the car to tell me where I am, and where I need to be.

All of us need that though. As I like to say, it is impossible to see your own face without a mirror, so you need something outside of yourself to let you know how you really look.

We need to be accountable to someone sometime. That is hard to do because it requires a certain amount of humility- a certain amount of vulnerability to another person to not only let them know where you are, but also where you need to go to get back on route. Unlike my naggy GPS, which always sounds angry with me when I get off route, we all need an accountability partner of some kind who will gently nudge us back on course. Of course, there are guys like me who sometimes need to get hit with a 2 x 4 in order to get it. Those are the kind of people I need in my life.

Who makes a good accountability partner? Finding a

mentor, a spiritual director, a good sponsor in a 12-step program, a brother or sister, a close friend or spouse, or heck, the whole community! (I think of those celebrities who go on public diets in order that the media actually becomes their accountability partner) I try and have a few accountability partners in my life- people I feel that I can trust and tell things to, who I know will not use it against me.

While we are growing up, our natural accountability partners should be our parents; and to a lesser extent our brothers and sisters. As those relationships change, as we get older, we have to make a conscious effort to find those accountability partners wherever we can.

The flip side of this coin is that when you become someone other people become accountable to, it really becomes a mutual relationship- a good accountability relationship goes both ways and benefits both people involved- a good teacher has to make sure they know their stuff! I know that people have trusted me in the past, and I ended up getting more out of the situation than they did in most cases!

Certainly no one is perfect, not even my GPS system which lead us astray the night we needed Java, but for the most part I trust that when I am off route, my GPS, and all the people who I have made myself accountable to in this life, will help me get back on.

Low Fuel Warning

So I was chatting with a friend of mine on the phone, and she mentioned that she ran out of gas on her way to work.

I am always stunned when people run out of gas, frankly, since most cars are equipped with low fuel warning lights to indicate that, well, you are low on fuel. That is what the light is for.

So I asked my friend, let's call her, Suzanne, "Suzanne, how do you run out of gas since there is a low gas light in your car?" I was both perplexed and fascinated. And a little hungry. That has nothing to do with this situation though. I just thought you might like to know.

Suzanne responded by saying that for some reason, the low gas light didn't come on in her car at all, so it was something of a shock to her as well. I imagine there was a feeling of dread as the car sputtered to a stop...

I know that in my driving career, I have let the gas light come on quite a few times. When you are out and about and on the road, it is an inconvenience to stop and fill up the gas tank, even though you know you need it, or the price at this station is 3 cents lower than any other station you have seen. I hate it when that little light comes on, because really, I have no choice. Within a few miles Lucy (my car) and I will be stranded on the side of the road. The little indicator light, when it is working, tells me that it is time to stop by and refuel. Unfortunately for Suzanne, that light failed her. I did tell her how good of an analogy this was, and how I wasn't going to give her any credit.

It is too bad that we don't come with "low fuel warning" lights. Lord knows I could use one. Back in the days before warning lights in cars, I bet it was much more common to have cars run out of gas. That little light, and the fuel gauge altogether tell us that it is time to refuel, or risk getting stranded on the side of the road.

For those of us without built in fuel lights, it is hard for us to know when our spiritual, emotional, or even physical tank is getting near empty. Certainly, like a fuel gauge in a car there are lots of indications that we are running on fumes, such as irritability, acting out with food or drugs or alcohol, insomnia, or even depressions. Like a fuel gauge though, it is very possible to ignore the obvious signs, and tell ourselves that we have plenty of gas left in the tank, and that if we drive even faster, we will get more out of what we have left.

Probably when our personal tanks get empty, it becomes something of an inconvenience to stop and refuel, just because we feel like we need to get where

A Cure For Heartburn
www.FatherWagner.com

we are going, and stopping for gas would just slow us down.

A stopped car never goes anywhere folks. Never…

All of a sudden we will stop. We will sputter, and we will be stranded on the side of the road, forced to call in help. This leads us to embarrassment, sorrow, and sadness. I imagine that even in a big city, getting stranded on the side of the road is one of the loneliest feelings that one can have; I imagine that the only thing worse is having your life get stranded on the side of the road as well.

We need to make sure that we are taking care of ourselves in every way, and that in the midst of our business in life, we aren't simply running near empty all the time. When a car gets stranded on the side of the road, it affects the traffic around it. Even if it is on the shoulder, the other cars will slow down, and look, forcing traffic itself to slow down. We have to remember that to take care of our basic human needs helps others to get where they are going as well, and not to affects everyone else in a negative way.

So it should not be seen as an inconvenience to stop and refuel. If it is important, we are going to do the things that we need to take care of ourselves and others- we will pray or meditate, we will stimulate ourselves intellectually, get enough sleep, eat right,

A Cure For Heartburn
www.FatherWagner.com

exercise, take time for friends and family, and simply stop and let the engine cool down a little. It doesn't take much- a car can run for hundreds of miles on one tank of gas, and it only takes a few minutes to fill up.

How full is your tank?

4th Grade Magic Show

When I was in 4th grade, I was really into magic- I mean really into it. I think it all started when my Mom took me to see David Copperfield (the illusionist, not the Dickens' character) the year that he walked through the Great Wall of China. (Incidentally I had a trick that performed a couple of times in High School that was similar- I could break the Great Chair of Aluminium without batting an eye just by sitting on it). (Not to mention futons)

In this particular show, DC didn't have a Great Wall of China to walk through, but he did have a somewhat impressive metal wall that he walked through. As I recall, the trick took about 20 minutes to perform altogether, but 19 minutes of it was David Copperfield dancing around the wall in a dramatic fashion. Maybe I was just into dramatic dancing. No... it was magic.

All I could think of back then was figuring out how the heck he did that, and how no wall would ever hold me back again. I can't tell you how many walls I tried to walk through after that. I can't tell you because I eventually passed out from hitting my head on various walls trying to walk through them. I don't remember 1985 at all.

I even went as far as going to a Magic Society

meeting.

OK even as much as I was into magic back then, the Magic Society proved to be creepy, even by 4th grade standards. Sure these guys could make pigeons come out of places where no pigeon should be, but I am pretty sure it warped their brains somehow. (I remember one creepy guy in particular) (Creepy). Most of these guys did not have the grace, nor the finesse of David Copperfield, although there was a lot of dramatic dancing going on at the meeting I went to. Maybe I just went to the wrong meeting.

This did not deter me in the least. Certainly I wasn't called to join the Magic Society as a 4th grader- these guys spent way too much time doing magic even for me. I got my first magic kit shortly thereafter- a Harry Blackstone Magic kit. For those of you who don't know, Harry Blackstone was the David Copperfield of the 70's. He was a great man. More mysterious than dramatic, I think he was a great magician. (Could have used more dramatic dancing though.)

I spent the next couple of weeks learning the various tricks- making balls disappearing under cups, card tricks, various tricks involving strings (which almost made me lose a finger once by the way) (Strings tied to tight can cut off the circulation in a child's finger I learned one day) (On my own finger)

After a couple of weeks I felt like I was ready to

perform. I had perfected about half the tricks, and thrown in a few dramatic dance moved to boot and I knew it was time. So I approached my 4th grade teacher Mr. Sunderland, who also let me run a banking business in class (I made lots of money that year) (For a 4th grader) and I asked him to let me perform.

Perform I did- I don't know if it was the dramatic dancing, or the quality of magic, but I was able to dazzle the other 4th graders. As I get older, I realize how easy it is dazzle 4th graders by the way. A couple of my tricks flubbed up, but for the most part my career as a 4th grade magician was off to a running start. It was my first and last show. I did do some card tricks for a waitress at Bob Evans a few weeks after that, but that was the end of my professional career before I found something else, or my banking business took too much of my time.

I think my interest in magic goes right along with a lot of my habits and actions. In sacraments class back in grad school in Rome, our professor told us the difference between magic and prophecy. Prophecy in a culture is for the good of the culture and not the prophet, whereas magic is an attempt to control one's environment- it is somewhat self-centered.

Who doesn't want to control their environment and walk through walls or fly around? If that sentiment wasn't shared by a lot of people there wouldn't be comic book heroes with superpowers, or people like Donald Trump and Martha Stewart. It is in our nature to try and control our environment however it is possible, and magic seems to do that well. It seems that David Copperfield can dance through a wall or make the statue of liberty disappear. It seems like he has total control over his environment when in reality it is all an illusion.

That is about the same when it comes to controlling our own environments- it is an illusion to believe that we have control over most of anything- that attempt to control our feelings or emotions or the actions of our environment of others is simply like magic- an illusion. There are lots of ways we try to do that by the way that are much more dangerous than magic- work, titles, power, drugs, alcohol, spending- insert your vice here. None of it gives us any more control over our environment than anything else. I often wonder, with all their money, how free someone like Donald Trump or Martha Stewart really is. Maybe they are slaves to their money- I would bet they are.

Realizing how little control we have over things is really liberating. I can't even control how I feel about things- I can't control how you feel about things- I can't change the weather or walk through walls. What I do have control over however, thanks to the grace of God, are my choices- my actions. I do have control over that no matter what is going on around me. I do not believe that we are necessarily determined to act in a particular way because of our environment or upbringing. I think often that we, myself included, simply choose to go with what is easier or comfortable or what we know thus giving our free will to someone else, or enslaving it to some kind of addiction. Certainly we are created to be free rational beings capable of entering into good relationships with other people of free will. It is hard to take back our free will because that means maybe ticking someone off, but you are probably going to tick someone off anyway, and you can't please everyone (another issue of control) so you might as well not try. The best thing to do is to try and do what is good and right in a particular situation.

The intelligent thing is to cultivate our free will- to learn to discern what is best for you and those around you, what is within your power to do, and to do that thing. I can't determine how anyone acts but me, and even then to act completely freely I need the grace of God himself to be the free being he created me to be.

Thermostat in my Car

A wise man once said- "Walk right side of road, squished like grape. Walk left side of road, squished like grape. Walk middle of road, you safe." That wise man: Mr. Myiagi from the <u>Karate Kid</u> series. He could also beat up guys half his age and twice his size- AND catch flies with chopsticks. Which go great, by the way, with a little soy sauce and Cantonese rice.

It is funny- I have never been the kind of guy to walk down the middle, although I am certainly learning. I am a guy that if I do something, I want to do it all the way and absolutely- giving everything I am and have to a particular pursuit. Sometimes that has worked out for me- like in school or in work, and other times it hasn't worked out so well for me.

A great analogy for who I am, and I suspect who a lot of people are, is the thermostat in my car. If it is hot outside, I always put the air-conditioner on full blast, fan all the way up, knob turned all the way to the cold side of the dial. I love getting it so cold in my car that you can see your breath and draw things on the frosted glass of the car. Personally, I don't think there is anything better than getting out of a cold car into a hot day.

Once it does get too cold for the yeti (or big foot as he

is commonly known in West Virginia, according to my friend Doug Ondeck) I don't merely turn the thermostat down- nope, I turn the fan all the way off. Then when it gets hot again, I turn the fan all the way on full blast. There isn't a lot of middle ground with me.

The same thing happens when it is cold outside. My car, the coolest car ever in the world, has a remote starter on it. So what I do is I start the car, making sure that the heat is all the way in the red part of the dial, and the fan is on 4. Then I set a lump of dough on the seat, and by the time I get out there, the car is so hot it can cook the lump of dough into bread. Who doesn't like fresh bread on their way to work? I know I do. Then I usually turn the heat all the way off. Not much middle ground there either.

I guess Mr. Myiagi is right though. I notice that I have done a lot of things like that in my life. Some have said that it is an all or none proposition with me. I suspect that there is a little area in everyone's life where it is all or none, or there is a lot of excess.

The Greeks defined virtue as the golden mean- walking down the middle of the road, not too much one way, or too much to the other but virtue is found in the middle- in moderation. That is something I am actually learning about in my life right now. You can in fact have too much of a good thing.

I think we should take the European view of life. If

A Cure For Heartburn
www.FatherWagner.com

you ever eat in France you know that their portions are never big- it is just enough to get a taste, and not enough of anything to fill you up (except for that one Christmas dinner I ate there. That is another story). Here in the States when you go to a restaurant the portions are so big, you usually need to get carried out on a stretcher! Thanks a lot Cheesecake Factory!

That is how life should be I guess. We should try and set the dial to something that is consistent- not too hot, not too cold.

I am actually trying to do that in my life right now. I notice that when I am in the car, the fan is on about 2 or 3 (out of 4) and the knob is set at a comfortable quarter point, never too hot or cold. I am trying to learn how to walk down the middle of the road so I don't get squashed like a grape.

Maybe you have something that is a little extreme in your life. The way that we move back into the center is to do it slowly and consistently. It is funny how when you work on one virtue, you discover that they are all connected and when you find the golden mean in one area of your life, you find it in others.

The Wise Fortune Cookie

Recently, I was out and about and got to try two very wonderful Asian Cuisines. One was Thai, and the other Chinese. Of course it was delicioso as they say in the old country... of... Europe. I always like to have a little spice in my food, and I ended up having the Hot Pepper Chicken for lunch, and the always-palatable General Tso's chicken for dinner. That General Tso must have been one spicy meatball! I believe that he defeated his enemies with flavor, and his army was made entirely of breaded chickens.

Eating either of these fine dishes requires Jedi like skills so that you don't accidentally ingest one of the little red peppers that rattle when your fork gets too near. Once my brother, Owen, was eating a bit of leftover Chinese food when his Jedi skills failed him and he ate one of those peppers whole. It was a great show as he guzzled down gallons of water to try and quench the fire that had erupted on his tongue. It sort of reminded me of the time Homer Simpson ate one of the hallucinating peppers in the famous episode of the chilli cook-off. I don't think my brother saw a coyote with the voice of Johnny Cash, but I am sure he would have said something if he had. He did, however, begin to howl like some kind of coyote after he ate the nasty little pepper.

One of the great things about eating Asian food is at the end you get the little fortune cookie. Actually, I can't stand Chinese food; I just go for the fortune cookies. (OK, that's a lie!) It would probably cost me a lot less to just go out and buy them wholesale, but I like the whole experience, and plus, you get free chopsticks.

I used to have a rule that you had to eat the cookie before you read your fortune or it wouldn't come true. Now that I have given up sugar, I have rescinded that rule, and just read the fortune. I got two fortunes yesterday, since I ate at two different places.

The first: "Don't let the past and useless details choke your existence."

(Lucky numbers 5, 14, 28, 7, 42,36)

It is possible for us to be choked by our past, and the decisions that we have made, which brings us to wherever we are now. I was with my Spiritual Director in Toledo, and we talked about the fact that God doesn't waste anything, and even if he uses circuitous methods for getting us where He wants us, nothing is ever wasted. So we should look upon our past decisions, both good and bad, as part of the path that leads us to where we are right now, which will lead us down that path of life in the future. We shouldn't regret the past, nor wish to shut the door on it, but learn to use it to make wise decisions in the future.

The other part of the fortune is that we shouldn't let the minor details, past, present, or future give us such anxiety that it "chokes" our existence. As a wise fellow once told, me, God is in the details, but we shouldn't get caught in such minutia that we miss the bigger picture, or life in general.

My second fortune told me: "An unexpected event will soon bring you fortune." (Lucky numbers 4,6,11,24,37)

It is my hope that this unexpected event will be that one of my readers will take these numbers, win the lottery, and share the money with me. Further, I will use my lottery money to buy more fortune cookies, which will in turn win me more lottery money. A perfect plan!!!

Running on Treadmills

I am a wimp.

It's official.

It is something that I have to admit to myself, my family, and complete strangers on the interweb... I am a wimp.

I took up running about 11 months ago or so on a dare... a bet... a challenge? Someone told me that it would be possible for me, Joshua Wagner, to run a half marathon- 13.2 miles. I scoffed and I sconed. Wait... a scone is a pastry. I may have had one of those though when they told me, as a reaction to the scoffing. I have scoffed with a scone, and I have sconed with a scoff. What the heck am I talking about?

So I began to train- training was a great experience of my life because I found out that I am not physically incapable of running. I hadn't done that since my triumphal days of winning the 5th grade high jump competition in Mrs. Thomas' gym class. Sure it was tough at first putting one dainty foot in front of the other- ok my feet are anything but dainty, but you get the point. I had to start training indoors though because of the afore mentioned wimpyness.

See, I hate the cold. I was never a big fan of it, even growing up on a farm in the frozen tundras of Lima,

Ohio. The only good thing cold is good for is bringing snow and cancelling school. That's it. Otherwise it just makes me downright irritable. And cold. It makes me cold. Now that is not to say that I don't like crisp- crisp is good…. I like being crispy in the fall when the wind is still, and you can wear a sweater. I just like to avoid being cold. Believe me, Phoenix, Arizona looks pretty good after about December 3rd.

So when I started training for the Marathon last year, I had to start training indoors because it was January- on treadmills. That was alright because I never knew any better- previous to January of last year, the furthest I ran was when Pizza Hut began their all you can eat Pizza buffet. I was customer number 3!

The nice thing about running on treadmills is that you can watch TV. I watched a whole season of <u>Thundercats</u>, the greatest cartoon of the 1980's on the treadmill. It is always good to have someone to run with, and my running partner was often Lion-O, leader of the Thundercats. Snarf. (Hey the spell check actually knows the word Snarf! That's just Smurfy!)

Then I got to go run on a track! WOW what an experience. It was like I was unfettered, unbridled, and free as a bird! The track I ran on seemed like I had been able to wake up from a long nap, after a cup of Hybernol, and be liberated from the incessant hum of the treadmill track.

Plus I could watch other people work out and play in the gym that I was running at. All was good with the world, and as April approached, so did the warm weather.

I began to run outside. There is nothing better than running outside- especially in the city. I prefer city running to forest running because there is always something new to see as you run in the city. To me, trees begin to look alike after awhile when I am running, and I get bored. I would often run with my arms stretched out toward the heavens, and hum the theme from "Chariots of Fire."

Now that it is getting cold again, and January is quickly approaching, it is time to start thinking about getting on a more rigorous training schedule again. But that means running on treadmills again while it is cold, and that is tough. After about 3 miles I just want to scream. Sometimes I do, and it freaks people out in the gym. (They asked me not to do that any more.)

It made me realize that running is much more than just putting one foot in front of the other- it is a whole experience, body, mind and spirit. I often saw running journals on the racks of news-stands, and I couldn't figure out how someone could publish a monthly magazine about something we do almost naturally. Running was one of the best things to take up, because I believe it is more of a mental sport than a physical one.

All sports are like that though- heck, anything is like that. The problem with treadmills isn't that it is physically harder to run, but that it is mentally harder to run- you aren't going anywhere it seems- that is hard to take psychologically I imagine, and I believe that 3 miles on the treadmill is always going to be harder than 10 miles outside.

One of the great lessons that running has taught me is that if you believe that you can do something, you will probably do it. If you think you will fail, you will probably find some way to fail. In some areas of our lives we need to re-tool the way that we think in order to achieve the good in our lives that we want.

When I run on treadmills I have to fool my mind by various tricks that I have learned. I cover the time and the distance with a towel, I play inspiring music, I envision myself running outside... although I would never recommend running on treadmill with your eyes shut for more than about two seconds... yikes!!

Crypto Zoology (Is it Yeti, Yet?)

Shhh…. be very quiet… we are hunting Sasquatch.

I am writing this from the great city of Charleston, West Virginia- the great home of… well… Um… Charleston Chew? I am here visiting my friend Doug, with my other friend Dave, two guys I went to school at.

As I am writing this, Doug is over my shoulder, judging my every word, and making sure that I get all the facts right. The first question I asked is, what is Charleston famous for… his answer… Charleston Chew. Is that like Big League chew Deek?

Deek is what we have called ol' Douger since we knew him- he is now living the "high life" in the heart of Charleston- we started calling him Deek because the Dean of Men in our college had an Uncle named Oscar Aloysius Umberg- AKA Deek. That name was ceremoniously passed on to Doug in my Sophomore year in memory of the original Deek.

Deek has many redeeming qualities- he is well studied and educated- a hard worker- intelligent and hilarious. OK none of that is really true, but he was standing over my shoulder as I typed that last sentence and I didn't want to hurt his feelings.

Of all the things that impress me about ol' Deek is his love for the sciences. Doug is not a scholar of your

A Cure For Heartburn
www.FatherWagner.com

traditional sciences though, like chemistry or biology. Nope. He is a student of the niche science of "crypto zoology."

Yea I didn't know what that was either.

Last night, once Dave and I arrived, we all settled down for a feast of cheeses, olives, and Wheat Thins. Those are something like a cracker, but more like a snack. We settled in for some conversation since we hadn't seen ol' Deek in a year. I decided to check out the selection on his DVR (digital video recorder), and all I saw was a show called <u>Monster Hunter</u>. I had never heard of that before, but it was on the <u>Discovery</u> channel, so I suspected that it was nothing but the highest quality science. It was all that was on his DVR.

I shrugged my shoulders and went on with the evening. Flipping through the channels, a live episode of the afore mentioned show came on and we watched it. They were searching for the Lock Ness monster.

Excited, Doug ran to his room to return with a veritable library of books about many crypto zoology topics such as Big foot (AKA yeti, AKA Sasquatch, AKA that guy I saw at the gym last week). Crypto zoology for us laymen, is the search for the strange beasts and creatures that clandestinely live among us without us know it. My friend Doug is a Crypto zoologist.

I was about to pack up my bags to go once he came out with all those books. I am not sure what I was more afraid of- the actual idea of Big foot, or the fact that my buddy believed that he was lurking about the streets of Charleston ready to strike us. (Turned out it was just a guy named Wade by the way).

Apparently there is a big industry for this stuff- books upon books have been written about creatures that apparently are smart enough to only have been filmed once in the whole last 75 years of film. From Lock Ness, to Yeti, to the dreaded "Moth man" there are all sorts of scary creatures that must be lurking just behind my back, ready to pester me.

Still I have to say, sometimes there are people that I know exist and I never see them. It is good to know my friend Doug continues to exist, even if we haven't seen each other in over a year.

It is funny, the three of us only get together sporadically, and yet, when we do get together it is like time never passes- we just pick up where we left off- same jokes and everything. I guess that is what true friendship is really all about- it will have a timeless quality that lets you not only accept the weird and quirky things about them (like being a certified crypto zoologist and searching for Big foot… weirdo) as well as the good things.

The ancient Greeks, specifically Aristotle believed that friendship is the highest form of relationship. There is nothing selfish about it- rather it is for the mutual up-building of each party involved. Friendship is also never exclusive- as CS Lewis says, it is always ready to bring more people into the fold.

So I guess since I am friends with these guys, I will put up with a little hunt for Yeti (which we actually did last December in the woods of Ohio) since I know they will sleep better at night knowing that Sasquatch is safely held in the mystical forest that he lives in with the Easter bunny and the tooth fairy.

A Cure For Heartburn
www.FatherWagner.com

Hostile Hostels

Man do I love to travel. Travelling, no matter if it is far or near is always a learning experience. I love going to new exotic locations, or re-visiting old ones that I have been to… it doesn't matter.

I always meet new and exciting people on my voyages, and thanks to years of experience living and travelling through Europe, I have a lot of know-how on how to make a travelling experience fulfilling, fun, and most importantly cheap.

Once upon a time, in a galaxy far away, I used to stay in Hostels. Oh, hostels. One step up from a Maytag refrigerator box really. The only hostel that I ever really liked was the hostel in Naples, Italy, ironically in the city that I liked the least. The best part of Naples was the hostel where you basically got your own room (with the exception of the other stranger living in there, but it was better than most.)

Once in Ireland I got stuck in Galway City, and so I went to a hostel.

Most hostels were just communal rooms with racks and racks of bunk beds, and smelled faintly (or not so faintly) of feet and body odor. Then there were the showers. You would think that as much as the showers were obviously used, the smell of feet and body odor would have been all but eliminated, but somehow it lingered. The showers, no matter what hostel you were in, were always covered in mildew, and always had about an inch of standing water. It didn't matter if you let it drain or not, or if you let the water run all morning, there was always an inch of murky white water, mixed with soap, shampoo, and whatever.

Sleeping in the communal hostel rooms was always fun too- it was always cold (and did I mention smelly?) I was always afraid of getting my stuff stolen (because who wouldn't want a collection of solid colored giant polo shirts from JC Penny?) so I slept in the rack with all my stuff pulled next to me.

Hostels were nice in the fact that they were ALWAYS cheap- less than 20 bucks a night, and you always met interesting people… and they became your best friends for about 3 days. You would eat together, travel together, then get mutually tired of each other, find another group to travel with, and go your separate ways, never to talk again. (Actually I did stay friends with a couple of people I travelled with for awhile).

Once in Galway City Ireland, I was supposed to meet some friends from school that I was going to travel with for the rest of the week. Unfortunately, my train from Dublin to Galway, which crosses the whole island, caught fire, making me about 6 hours late. (By the way… buses in Ireland folks, not trains.) So upon arrival I mosied my way up to a nice looking hostel and I checked in. I was shown to my room, a smaller communal room with about 4 bunk beds. A relative paradise to the huge communal hostels I had stayed in before.

I was tired and needed a shower, so I began to prepare. All of a sudden a pretty girl walked into the room I was staying in. Usually in the smaller hostels, they would separate men from women, so I thought this was an odd occurrence that she was in my room. We exchanged pleasantries, and I learned that she would be occupying the top bunk in the bed I had chosen. Perplexed, I asked her if I was in the wrong place, and she casually said no. I believe she was Canadian. Maybe Canadians are cool with that sort of stuff.

So I got my shower gear together, and walked over to the shower room- the girl was right behind me, and again I was perplexed that she followed me in. (A little flattered, mostly nervous...) I casually checked the door, which simply said "shower." I went into one stall, she into the other. Again, maybe Canadians are cool with that.

With a sense of propriety I got ready for my shower in the little ante-chamber which was about 4 foot by 4 foot. I am a big guy- it was sort of like that scene from <u>Tommy Boy</u> when he is trying to change clothes in the air plane lavatory. I was terrified that I was going to fly out of there in front of everyone, and all I could think of was the uncomfortable showering situation that I had unwittingly found myself. I was nervous to say the least. I was also nervous to see my pal "one inch of murky water," waiting for me in the shower.

I got done with my bid-ness and got completely dressed in the shower, socks, shoes, everything, before I went out. If I had a burka, I would have worn it. I decided to go for a walk, where, thank goodness, I ended up running into my friends. I checked out of the most liberal hostel in the universe, thankful that I didn't have to sleep in some weird co-ed situation.

 While hostels would not suit me any more, I have to say that they were always an interesting part of my travelling experience. You would meet people from all over the world, with different beliefs and ethnicities, backgrounds and stories, and then you would shower with them. If the world were like a hostel, maybe it would be a better place. Nah… I would just prefer to have my own shower.

Hospitable Hotels

In the previous chapter, I made mention of one of my harrowing experiences in a hostel in the middle of Galway City, Ireland. Every single time you walked into a hostel, you never knew what to expect. Once, in a hostel in Bologna, (mmm… bologna) I got into an argument with a fellow about the nature of Jesus Christ (the fellow was a Muslim by the way) which ended up getting him very upset by the end of the conversation. Seems he had some opposition to the fact that I held Jesus was the Son of God, and not simply a prophet as their religion believes. He got so angry that he got up, stormed out of room and went upstairs to his bed. I just sort of sat there and was glad that he left. About 20 minutes later, it was time for me to go to bed as well… I was somewhat concerned when I got up to my room, and saw that the guy sleeping across from me was my Muslim friend from downstairs. He gave me the ol' stink eye, he did.

I don't remember sleeping much that night. (That is not to say Muslims are bad folks by the way… one of my good friends in the city of Rome was a Moroccan named Habib, who took pictures of tourists around town with his Polaroid camera and sold them for 5 bucks.)

That was pretty much the end of my hostel career (although I believe there may have been one more in Sicily, which was a great wonderful experience altogether), as I began to graduate to hotels.

I enjoy hotels quite a bit actually... always have. Dateline, NBC almost ruined them for me when they started taking black lights through all the rooms and showing how clean (or not clean) "nice" hotels sometimes are. Makes me feel extra good about the murky waters of the hostels I stayed in. Maybe that is why my feet itch so bad sometimes. Um... anywho...

There are three points of travelling that I absolutely love, no matter where I am going or how long I will be gone. The first is the departure- there is that euphoria of adventure that is right around the corner- you never know what is going to happen- sure you have plans, but you are leaving behind your old world- all your "baggage," and escaping to a wonderful, unknown place, to meet new and exciting people. There is always a sense of having the weight lifted off of your shoulders as you leave it all behind.

The second point is actually arriving in a new hotel. The whole universe is in order when you get to a new hotel room. The beds are made, glasses are cleaned, the towels are hung perfectly on the rack. There is a sweet smell in the air- this is your little space in the world that is perfect and orderly. Plus there is a brand new set of channels to learn on the TV. Sure I have all the same channels at home on cable or satellite or whatever, but part of the adventure is figuring out where they are now. I will watch shows that I would otherwise just flip past when I am in a hotel room.

Then there is the heating and cooling system- another advantage over hostels. (Hostels are always cold. Summer, winter, fall... always cold.) In a hotel you can put the AC to sub freezing temperatures, or hot enough that the Devil himself couldn't stand it. I think there is nothing better than putting the AC on "frozen tundra" setting, and then getting under the piles of covers, surrounded by pillows. (Actually, a lot of hotels cover the beds with tons of pillows now, making fort building a real possibility in most hotels.)

Hotels are always new too- no matter how long you stay in one, when you leave, it is all magically back in order when you get back. There is always something to look forward to when you are staying a hotel. They clean up your life for you- all you have to do is enjoy the mint.

It is fun to get away every so often. I believe putting yourself into a new environment gives you a great idea of who you truly are. It is uncomfortable in its new comforts- you get to see how you really react in new situations. Hotels are a little break too from the usual rhythm of life. It would be nice to be able to live a life where all you do is move around to clean and orderly rooms, never letting your problems catch up with you. Plenty of people try to do that, by the way, with all sorts of things. There is no such thing as a geographic solution to a spiritual problem. They always catch up with you. Still, the break is nice every so often.

It gets tiring to run from your problems all the time though- because no matter how much you run from room to room, no matter how many times the cleaning staff comes in to turn down the bed, or how many TV's you learn the channels to, life will always catch up with us, and we will again have to deal with it.

That is the third most favorite part of any trip that I like to take- going home. When I am done with a trip, all I want to do is to get home. It is a different sort of anticipation from the feeling when you are leaving. As much as it is fun to get away and see new surroundings, it is always nice to go home where people, places, and things are familiar. When you come back though, you come back re-invigorated, and ready to take on those challenges of life.

It would be nice to stay on the mountain all the time, free from the rigours of life, but that isn't life. We can't hide from it- rather we have to take it head on. I think I would get tired really quick of having to learn a new set of TV channels every single day, but every once in a while it helps me to appreciate the ones I already know.

Snooze... Snooze... Snooze... Snooze... Snooze... Snooze... Snooze... Snooze... Snooze... Snooze... (get it?)

Holy Moly... I love my snooze button. Always have... always will. Well I have to really say that it is a love/hate relationship in the end. There are very few pleasures in life that are as good as the first time you try it: good dessert, a trip to a city, a movie. The snooze button though? Always... ALWAYS a pleasure. I imagine it is the next best thing to that little morphine button they give to patients in the hospital. And probably just as addictive.

Who doesn't love to indulge a little in the snooze button now and then? I set my alarm clock earlier than I want to get up so that I can hit the snooze. I am pretty sure some kind of wonderful dopamine is released every time I smash my hand down on that little alarm clock.

First, you get to kill something annoying. At least with my alarm clock you do. I bought this alarm clock for $4.99 at Wal-Mart. A sweet deal if you ask me. It has THE most annoying alarm clock sound in the whole world. I consider myself a word smith, and there isn't an apt description of just how bad this alarm clock is. I have considered throwing it across the room sometimes. Instead, I get to swat at it like some annoying bug in my room. You know that feeling of satisfaction you get from accurate swatting a housefly with a fly swatter? I know you know what I am talking about- that little rush of adrenaline- that feeling of accomplishment... I am getting goosebumps just thinking about it.

(As a side-note, the only thing more annoying that the sound of my current alarm clock was that week in College when I woke up to my radio instead, and that whole week they played Dave Matthew's band songs. Boy, that was some great snooze buttoning. This is the reason I hate Dave Matthews. Plus he tried to kill me. That is another story.)

So you get your little rush of dopamine- a feeling of euphoria sweeps through my entire body, and THEN you get to go back to sleep!!!! For 9 whole minutes! And how about that sleep? That 9 minutes of sleep in between snooze button hits is better than the 6 or 8 hours you might have gotten the night before. You get to stay in that half awake, half asleep place where everything is timeless. It seems like that 9 minute stretch feels at times like 20 minutes or half an hour. I have come up with some of my best ideas during that nine minutes of reprieve.

The best part is... you get to do it again after 9 minutes! SWAT... Euphoria... timeless half-sleep... SWAT... Euphoria... timeless half-sleep. I can possibly say that the snooze button is the greatest

invention that the 20th century has given us. Nope...
not the air plane or the computer... the snooze button.
What did our ancestors ever do? Wake up with the
sun? You can't swat that! I've tried! It is a giant ball
of fire, and it is millions of miles away!

It turns out though that I might have a problem. I
might be a snooze-button junky. Might is not the
proper word. I am Josh Wagner, and I am a snooze
button junky. There. Now the whole world knows. I
will stand up and admit it. I had to take certain steps
to solve this problem. I have been known to hit that
stupid button for more than a couple of hours. I
mean it would have been easier to just reset the clock,
but I would have missed all the fun of the snooze
button.

So here is what I did. I moved the clock into the next
room over. Thanks to the piercing sounds of the
alarm clock, it shoots right through the walls and into
my cerebellum. Dogs are awakened miles away by
the reverberations of my alarm clock. This requires
me to get out of bed- walk into the next room THEN
hit the snooze button. I still get the dopamine, and
the timeless sleep, but by the third hit, I am pretty
much awake enough to realize I have to go to the
bathroom. (Too much info? Truth too hard to take?
You can't handle the truth!)

I realized that I had a problem a long time ago, and I
knew that the solution would be to move the clock,

A Cure For Heartburn

but it took me three weeks to do it. I think it works that way with a lot of things in life. A lot of times we know that there is a problem or an addiction or what-have-you, but it sometimes takes us months or years to actually try and find a solution to our particular issue. It is just easier to live with the trouble sometimes than to try and fix it.

I certainly don't enjoy my new-found solution to my snooze button fix, but it is better for me. After moving my clock I am awake and refreshed, and I can start my day- I am fully awake- not just crawling out of bed, but springing out of bed, a new pep in my step! (Hey that was a clever rhyme huh?!)

Sometimes, the solutions to our problems seem worse than the problem itself, but in the long run, when we realize that there is something that is taking our ability to fulfil our potential away, a little bit of pain and sacrifice aren't a bad thing at all. Neither is giving up something today that will benefit us in the long run.

I guess there are two themes here. The first is habit- not all habit is good, even if it is pleasant. There are a lot of analogies we can make to the alarm clock example- something that seems pleasant, but can ruin your whole day and make you lethargic. Something we know we need to change, but it is hard and requires a lot of will power (and grace). It means that we have to admit to ourselves that we need the help of someone greater than ourselves in order to restore us to right order. That can be hard for a lot of people, because that means taking a critical look at themselves and admitting that there is something that needs fixed or at least attention in their lives. That is hard for a lot of people to admit- to admit that they in fact aren't perfect.

The second theme is procrastination. Boy that is a problem isn't it? I had a terrible time with that in college (and sometimes still do!) We know we have to do something- we know it is the right thing- and still we put it off. Maybe we put it off because it is hard or will take a lot of time and energy, much like trying to change a habit. Or maybe we put it off because we are afraid that we might fail at it. That is easy to do.

A solution to this problem of procrastination that I have found is to write down the goal, set a date and a time to do it, and get yourself mentally and spiritually ready to do it. I myself have to get geared up sometimes to take on a big project or effect some change in my life. Sometimes I just need someone to kick me in the rear to get started. Don't be afraid to ask for that type of help.

Good things in life are good if they aren't overused… the second that the snooze button begins to control us, we begin to lose who we authentically can become.

Changin' My Oil...

I was driving around the other day minding my own business, trying to fight the dreary dank of central Ohio, when I glanced up at my wind shield and saw that pesky little sticker that tells me it was time to change my oil. I looked at the date, and according to that, I have plenty of time before I need to take ol' Lucy in for an oil change. A sign of relief escaped my lips, and I turned up the stereo. Then I looked back at that little sticker in my wind shield, and saw the mileage part of the sticker: it read 31,268 miles. I looked at my odometer. 32,535 miles.

Thanks to my Dad, I am one of those really scrupulous drivers that the oil companies love: I always try to change my oil every 3500 miles or so. I love my car (as you may know) and I think it is worth 30 bucks every couple of months to give Lucy a transfusion. Maybe it is in my head, but I think she runs better when I do that.

I recalled one of my brothers that had troubles with cars in the past. He shall remain nameless (although I only have three brothers, so I guess it wouldn't be hard to narrow it down.) Many years ago, when he was a less responsible young man, he had a very nice Audi. Rarely, if ever, did he change the oil in that car. You know maybe this is the reason I change my oil so often- this traumatic experience has changed my life forever.

That car never ever ran right- it always sputtered or jerked or sounded funny. Are care supposed to make a crunching sound when they go past 30 MPH? This one did. One day, as I recall, I was in the car with my brother when the car just completely stopped and locked up. It started smoking. It smelled of old burned oil. Something wasn't right.

I don't remember the Audi too long after that. Moment of silence for the car.

...

Still being silent...

...

And we're done.

I think that people are a lot like cars- there are a lot of different parts that have to work together for our lives to go smoothly. If we begin to neglect even one of those important parts, it is going to wear on the other parts of the car- if the engine doesn't work right, the wheels aren't going to be going anywhere. If you

A Cure For Heartburn
www.FatherWagner.com

have bad tires, the engine is going to have to work overtime to move the car etc.

To really maintain a car in road worthy condition you have to make sure all the parts of the car are in working order. The same with us. If our spiritual life is out of whack, then our health might also be out of whack. If our social life is in the dumps, it may affect our working life. Life is really about finding out what the little thumps and knocks are in our lives, and fixing the problem. Sometimes that is simple as "changing our oil."

There are lots of ways to do that- sometimes it is as simple as scheduling some time out for ourselves (and yes, sometimes you do have to schedule it). Maybe it is going on a retreat, or a long drive. Maybe even hitting a few golf balls or calling a friend. Taking care of yourself in these most important areas of your life is not selfish. In fact, it is the very opposite! How can you take care of the people you love in your life if you are yourself a wreck?

I think a lot of people try and change their oil on their own, and if they know what they are doing, that is OK. I don't know what I am doing- if I were to change my own oil, I would probably mess up the car. Likewise, I need to find people and supports outside of myself- spiritually, socially, and even physically that can help me to change the oil in my life. Again, there are a variety of "garages" out there that can help us to change our oil so that our lives run smoothly.

You know, if would be nice to have an "engine light" or a mileage sticker for our lives to let us know when we need to change oil, but it unfortunately doesn't work that way. It is really easy to let one part of our life slip away and deteriorate, and before we know it, we are sitting stalled out in the intersection of life, smoking and burning oil.

The Modern Day Coliseum

When I was living in Rome, I used to do some tour guiding around the city so that I could afford a random plate of pasta, or a crust of bread every now and then. It was a tough life. One of the best things about guiding was that I got to meet interesting people, and know lots about interesting places. I would offer free tours to English speakers, make them laugh, tell them things about the sites that they didn't know (and sometimes I didn't know) and at the end I told them that if they liked my tour, and wanted to give me a gratuity, I would gladly accept it. I then told them that if they didn't I hope they got hit by the 64 bus. OK I never said that last part... but maybe I thought it every so often. Most people either liked my tours enough to give me some money, or they just sort of felt guilty because I made that statement with the saddest puppy dog face that I could make. It was pretty pathetic.

Anyway, one of my favorite places to tour was the Coliseum in Rome. When you go there, you can't help but be mesmerized by the magnificence of the structure of the Coliseum. The high archways, the impressive passages, the fact that there is really nothing but gravity holding the whole thing together.

All of modern Rome buzzes around this ancient structure as if it weren't even standing there. Amazing.

The Coliseum, along with the Circus Maximus, were the entertainment center of ancient Rome. For almost half the year there would be spectacles for people to watch ranging from wild animals brought all the way from Africa to be slaughtered in front of the crowds, to mockeries of midgets and "giants" (of which I would qualify at 6 3" by the way), and of course the gladiator competitions. Gore, and conflict were the life breathe of the coliseum's daily activities, and tens of thousands of people would flick in day after day to witness it. (By the way, my favorite part of my tour of the Coliseum was the so-called vomitoriums, which were basically drainage pipes that people would, well, throw up in, when the gore got to them. Those Romans thought of everything).

I can only imagine the roar of the crowd in the midst of these blood sports, how they were driven into a frenzy each and every time something dramatic happened.

Then just over the Thanksgiving Holiday, I was flipping through the channels, and I happened upon the Jerry Springer show. I knew what it was like to watch the gore and the mayhem of the Coliseum 2000 years ago.

The same thing was happening- midgets and giants

were literally being made fun of. Male and female gladiators, now wearing flannel shirts and miniskirts instead of armor, wrestled each other to the ground in an epic battle. Again the crowd roared with delight at the spectacle that had formed on the stage, and Jerry, the ringmaster of this sick circus stood proudly watching. Luckily, I was at the end of the show, and it was over all too soon with a little bit of "wisdom" from Jerry Springer right before Maury Povich came on with his daily paternity test results.

I guess in some respect human nature hasn't changed that much in 2000 years since the glory days of the Coliseum in Rome. I would wager that this sort of thing didn't jump 20 centuries either from the Coliseum to the stage of Jerry Springer. People have always been emotional voyeurs, in the sense that they like to see the pain and suffering of other people- it can drive them into a frenzy.

I don't think it is any different when it comes to following people like Brittany Spears, or Anna Nicole Smith, or when a political scandal arises because some Senator tapped his foot in an airport restroom. Those things sell- and they sell for the same reason that people bought tickets to the Coliseum or the Jerry Springer show.

I think it makes us feel better- I will admit in college watching a few Springer episodes and laughing at the poor people that were making fools of themselves (real or fake) on that stage in Chicago. It makes us feel better about our own lives and our own problems and situations. At least we aren't as bad as these people, or moreover, we don't have it as bad as these people.

It is nice to see people like Brittany or Anna Nicole fall too- these are the stars- the royalty of our own culture and society. If they can have all this fame and money, and still have lives worse than ours, it does make us feel better about our own troubles.

I guess I have changed in the last few years- I am not entertained by this sort of pointless suffering any more. It makes me feel bad for people who are on Jerry Springer, or who are famous and panned, or who are even gossiped about at the water-cooler at work. Nobody is perfect, and what we really need to do is to focus on our own personal crosses, to carry them with the strength of God, and to help others carry their crosses where and when they can, rather than mocking them for how distorted or heavy their own crosses may be in order to forget our own.

SIN

Ohhh… people get creeped out by this topic don't they? Nobody wants to be known as a sinner- yet I have yet to meet one perfect person in this world, especially the guy that stares back at me in the mirror. Admittedly, I am ALMOST perfect, but I still have a week or two before I reach perfection.

Sin is not a word that is commonly used in our culture. It is imperative that we hide the fact that we are sinners at all costs, and let no one see our flaws, and the fact that we sometime fall short. In short, not only is there a misconception of what sin is, it isn't even something that most people worry about. Sometimes I think we speak about morality and ethics as a sort of balance or an equation. Namely, if I do 8 good things, and 2 bad things, I am still a "good" person, and it somehow balances out. It's funny though, I don't remember a lot of good things sometimes- I often remember the bad things that I have done. We always remember the bad things.

The other problem with sin, and I think that this is why we tend to stray away from the concept of sin altogether, is that we feel ashamed about it- that is probably natural. What is worse about this is that it can be, and is, used to control us or other people. It is sort of like poking a bruise on someone's arm and not stopping until they do whatever it is that we want. The rest of the body can be healthy, but it is that one tender spot that we will guard and protect, simply because we know it can be used against us.

I think we need to take a good look at what sin is, and how it can be used TOWARD GOOD in our lives and the lives of others. I think that a lot of people's notion of sin is very immature. I know mine has been up until recently.

I was speaking with my spiritual director and this topic came up. It came up because I deal with guilt and shame and sin just like everyone else does. My sense of sin, and therefore of love, is currently under a lot of development so it comes up a lot in our conversations. I guess I will return to the effect that sin has had in my own life and reckoning.

As we talked about things, my Spiritual Director, a wise man in many many respects of human nature, told me that there are three levels of sin that we must pass through. He also told me that most people don't get out of the first one. So I think it would be a good idea to write about these three levels of sin. I think it will surprise people where this takes us, simply because most people's concept of sin is so basic.

At its base, sin, at least the theological concept of it in the west, is based on a legal concept in Judaism, which later gets translated in some respects, at least in theory (but often not practice). That concept is, in

A Cure For Heartburn
www.FatherWagner.com

Greek, Hamartia. Hamartia literally means to "miss the mark." Sort of like shooting darts and missing the bullseye. Of course, this is not exhaustive of the concept of sin, but it is a good starting point. Some people are good at darts, and some aren't, but nobody hits the bullseye every time. So when we "sin" we miss the mark that we are aiming for.

So that brings us to the question- what is the mark we are aiming for? I believe that this is the concept that changes as time goes on, and as we mature psychologically and spiritually. That is IF we mature psychologically and spiritually. I know from my recent experiences in life that I am not anywhere close to where I should be in those areas.

The three stages of our concept of sin are infantile, adolescent, and adult, or mature. I don't think a lot of people get past the first one. Maybe I am just reading into it though, because until recently my concept of sin wasn't much better than the first one.

Infantile: The Old Testament had a lot of infantile concepts of sin. Basically, it is violation of prohibition- not doing the right thing… "being bad." I think that this is the popular notion of sin. It is how little kids are supposed to be able to tell right from wrong- Mom and dad say don't do this, and if the kid does it, he or she gets in trouble. This is the moral code of the Old Testament and the Law as well- don't do this or else. (Thou shalt not...). I think that this is a good natural development of sin that we should all go through, but I think that we stop there- it is easy to stop there and not go on simply because it is hard to go on to the other, more mature concepts of sin. It is good for people to keep their kids or loved ones, or spouses or employees at this level of a concept of sin, because it is black and white and easy to control and manipulate. It is also easy to make someone feel bad about themselves when all they have is this level of sin- people have been doing since the foundations of civilization. I know that personally, I was stuck in this concept of sin until recently, even though I knew better- I didn't do things out of motivation of love, but rather out of fear of punishment.

Adolescent: Our concept of sin should change as we grow older, but again for a lot of folks I don't think it does. Adolescence, which my spiritual director said is anywhere from 12-32, is a time of self discovery- a time to figure out who we are on the way of understanding who we are designed to be. Thus our concept of sin should also change- instead of simply avoiding what is prohibited, the sin of adolescence is in-authenticity- that is, not being who we are authentically meant to be. Not living up to our potential, or even attempting to- to be untrue to ourselves and not being authentically ourselves. This requires a development of self-identity that is difficult in this day and age- simply because it is easier to avoid prohibition than it is to develop an identity and live up to that identity.

Mature or adult: This is the ultimate notion of sin I believe. I think a few of us truly get to this level- it is hard and requires a choice rather than a feeling to avoid. The sin of adulthood is not simply prohibition, nor is it not "being yourself," rather it is missing opportunities to love. Mother Theresa once said that the worse sins are the sins of omission- that is missed opportunities to love. That is what the first sin is characterized in the Bible for instance- we often blame Eve for the first sin, but truly the first sin is that Adam had an opportunity to give his life in love for his spouse, his neighbor, and he failed to do so. If love is the willing the good of another, then sin really is the choice not to do so. It is a not simply doing what is prohibited, but not going the extra mile for the good of ourselves and our brothers and sisters no matter who they are.

My Spiritual Director pointed out the clearest example of this in the story of the Good Samaritan- all those people passed him by when he was mugged on the road because they were prohibited to touch him by the law or their inability to be the neighbor God designed them to be- it was the Samaritan who truly willed the good of the man who was robbed- he took

A Cure For Heartburn

the opportunity to love.

This is not necessarily a Christian concept, although it is highlighted by Christianity- Remember all theology, philosophy, and any science is there to highlight who we are in relationship to the rest of the cosmos. As rational creatures of free will, we have the innate ability to love- it is something that is in our nature- to will the good of another. Willing something is a rational choice, and a person that is mature understands that relationship to others, no matter what their background. As relational beings by nature, we are obligated not only to avoid bad and embrace good, but to be what our nature authentically directs us to be, and to will that others achieve the fullness of their potential as well.

A Cure For Heartburn
www.FatherWagner.com

Superman and Clark Kent

Maybe this is a well known fact, or maybe it isn't, but after this book gets to the rest of the world, it WILL be a known fact- wait… what am I talking about again? Anyway… it is a little known fact that in every Seinfeld episode, the Man of Steel, Superman, makes some kind of appearance in the background. Often he is on Jerry's refrigerator, or perhaps sitting in statue form on the shelf in the background, but he is always there. Jerry Seinfeld was always a big Superman fan.

That is at least one thing that Jerry and I share in common- namely that I am also a big Superman fan. I always have been ever since I saw Christopher Reeve fly across the screen in the first Superman movie when I was a kid. Who wouldn't think that Superman is cool? He can run fast, he can fly, he can shoot LASERS out of his eyes! That isn't all of course! This is why Superman has endured as an American Icon for more than 50 years now. He is sort of what every American envisions themselves as in a way- strong and capable of always following truth, justice, and the American way.

Maybe this is why when Christopher Reeve got hurt riding horses a few years ago we were all so interested. This was a guy who, in our minds, embodied all of those traits that we have come to love in Superman. All of a sudden a man that we equated with strength and valour and courage was sitting in a wheelchair, unable to move his arms and legs-struggling at times to breathe. Probably thousands of people suffer these sorts of injuries every day- why was he so important? I think at the point he had his accident it had been years since his last Superman movie, and a while since he had done any sort of movies that bear remembering. It was a tragedy not only for him and his family, but in a way for all Superman fans. It reinforced the fact that it was all an illusion, and that the man behind the giant "S" was just that- a man.

I think that there are other things to be fascinated about Superman, beyond the actor that played him once upon a time. The whole relationship of Clark Kent to Superman is always an interesting one as well.

What we have to remember from the story of Superman is that while he was given all the abilities that I mentioned above, developed through exposure to our yellow sun over his years on Earth, his first identity was not as Superman, but as Clark Kent.

As you may recall, Clark was raised by a farmer and his wife in Smallville after they found his pod crash landed in a field. From that point he had a normal childhood relatively speaking until his powers developed later in life. But his identity was firmly established as Clark way before he could fly or see through things.

I was always curious as to why he even kept up his Clark Kent persona at all. Why not just stay Superman all the time? Why not just keep the suit on? Why did he have to cover up the suit? Who was the real guy? Was it Clark Kent or was it the Superman that everyone saw? His powers and his beliefs were the same whether he was wearing the suit or not, so why the two personalities?

When he was Clark Kent, he always fumbled around-he wasn't smooth with Lois Lane, and while he was a good reporter for the Daily Planet, I suspect that he spent most of his time as Clark trying to live a relatively normal life. I mean, can you imagine the pressures of always having to be there for everyone all the time? I am sure he loved to get up in the morning, put on his Superman suit, and over the top of it his white shirt and tie. I am sure he loved being normal, and tried to do that. The real person underneath it all was the boy from Smallville, not the Superhero that everyone thought was there.

I think it was possible for him to put on the suit and play the character- he had the powers to do it, but if you ever read any of the comics, or watch any of the movies, it was a hard thing for Clark to do- he was always Clark- he was ALWAYS Clark. He was an

A Cure For Heartburn
www.FatherWagner.com

extremely conflicted character, because in one respect he had the physical ability to do so much good, but at the same time he had feeling and emotions just like the rest of us. I am sure that the people who only new him as Superman didn't understand that. I am not sure that I would expect them to either.

I remember my favorite Superman was Superman II. That was the one where he gave up his super powers for awhile to be with Lois. Really it was an analogy for the interior conflict that was within Clark- as the Superman part went off drinking and carousing, and the Clark Kent part went back to getting beat up in diners by truckers. At the end the Clark persona ends up fighting the Superman persona, merging them back into one super conflicted person again.

This might be the battle that Superman just can't win. Maybe it is his Kobyashi-Maru.

It is funny, sometimes we think that if we put on the Superman suit we will be able to fly. Sometimes we think that just because we have certain abilities, or attain a certain status, the internal conflict that we have endured our whole lives will magically disappear. It doesn't. In a way, the scene in the junk yard in Superman III is what we really have to do in ourselves- to struggle between what we are and what we are expected to be, either by ourselves or others.

Maybe when we put on the Superman suit, and then fail to fly, the first person that we disappoint is

A Cure For Heartburn

ourselves. Then we disappoint other people around us when we can't live up to the expectations that we helped to give them. I once had a professor in College reminds us that "Clothes mark the man, they don't make the man."

Clark's act was pretty good you know. It doesn't mean that he was insincere in pursuing truth and justice, but as Superman he couldn't let them see the interior weakness that he really had- he had to be all things to all people. I am sure it was a constant strain on his emotions- which put the strain on his ability to be the superhero everyone expected him to be. I imagine it is very difficult to be Superman when you know that despite your abilities and gifts, you really are weak on the inside, and you can't let people see that. Somehow Superman lived with that inner struggle.

Sometimes I wish I had Superman's abilities.

A Cure For Heartburn
www.FatherWagner.com

Made in the USA
Charleston, SC
12 April 2013